JUDGING FENCES
FOR CROSS COUNTRY

JUDGING FENCES FOR CROSS COUNTRY

Nina Lowe

Illustrated by the author

J. A. Allen
London

British Library Cataloguing in Publication Data
A catalogue record for this book is available from the British Library

ISBN 0.85131.592.5

Published in Great Britain by
J. A. Allen & Company Limited
1 Lower Grosvenor Place
London SW1W 0EL

© J. A. Allen & Co. Ltd.

Printed in Hong Kong by
Dah Hua Printing Co. Ltd.

Typeset in Hong Kong by Setrite Typesetters Ltd.

Designed by Nancy Lawrence

CONTENTS

FOREWORD

I am delighted to welcome this very accurate and well written guide to fence judging.

Whether at Pony Club, Riding Club, Novice or Advanced Horse Trials or at the major Three-Day Events, Fence Judges are a vital part of our sport. Sometimes they may sit all day in the rain judging a 'boring' fence; occasionally their accurate judgement will decide the destination of an Olympic medal.

Nina Lowe's enjoyable exposition of the art and science of judging will be enormously helpful to both experienced and new Judges. I hope it may also open some competitors' eyes to the debt they owe the volunteers who man obstacles every weekend.

When I am lucky enough to be a BHS Steward or an FEI Technical Delegate, I know that above all the experience and quality of the fence judging will determine how easy my job will be. Give me Nina and Ron Lowe at every fence and my job is redundant!

Hugh Thomas
Director, Badminton Horse Trials
Course Designer, Seoul Olympic Games 1988
Technical Delegate, Atlanta Olympic Games 1996

ACKNOWLEDGEMENTS

The author would like to thank the British Horse Society Horse Trials Group at the British Equestrian Centre for their help and support while this book was being written. I would also like to thank all those BHS Officials, Fence Judges, Organisers, Owners and Competitors, both past and present, who have given me so much helpful advice and support during my 'career' as a Fence Judge.

A big thank you, too, to Janet and Brian Hill of *Eventing Magazine* who published my series of articles on fence judging which was a forerunner to this book.

Last, but not least, my gratitude to my husband, Ron, who patiently word-processed the manuscript from my handwritten notes, and has been the best co-judge, complete with whistle and rake, that anyone could ask for!

Nina Lowe
Tunbridge Wells, 1993

INTRODUCTION

Horse trials originally began as a military sport as a means of testing the obedience, stamina, agility, speed and jumping ability of cavalry horses. After the second world war civilians were allowed to enter the competition, although it was only around 1950 that they came into the sport in any number. Since then, horse trials, or eventing as it is also called, has become an increasingly popular and fast-growing equestrian sport. This is reflected in the growing number of events which are organised each year, the long lists of riders who compete, and the crowds of spectators who attend.

Eventing is the all-round test of horse and rider. The competition combines dressage and showjumping with the speed and endurance section which at the highest level includes a steeplechase course and roads and tracks as well as the cross-country phase. The distance and the number of jumping efforts that the average horse is expected to make over the cross-country course increases with each level of event. A Pre-Novice course is 1600 m to 2800 m in length with 15–21 jumping efforts, while a four-star International Three-Day Event may have 45 jumping efforts over a distance of 7980 m. Heights, spreads and drops of fences become greater with each grade of competition.

The intention of this book is to discuss in detail the responsibilities of the Fence Judge on the cross-country phase. Obstacles on the course are solid and fixed and Fence Judges are assigned to each one. At Three-Day Events judges are also required for the fences on the steeplechase course. The development of this tough and competitive sport has meant that cross-country courses have become more complicated and technically demanding, particularly at advanced levels. The advice which I offer applies to all levels of competition from the local Pony Club Trial to the International Three-Day Event.

One of the main responsibilities of the Fence Judge is to judge and mark competitors at the obstacle. The rules are different depending on the type of competition so that there are separate rules for Official Horse Trials, Hunter Trials, and Pony Club and Riding Club Events.

The Fédération Equestre Internationale (FEI) lays down the rules and conditions under which all International Three-Day Events are conducted. The FEI was formed in 1921 after an International Congress had met to work out a complete set of rules which would be uniformly applied in every country. The rules for national competitions are set by the respective National Federations and have some changes and variations while keeping to the spirit of the FEI rules. In Britain, One- and Two-Day Events are run under the rules of the British Horse Society (BHS).

The FEI and BHS rules are straightforward. However, it is surprising how many interpretations and misconceptions there are. I intend to offer some clarification of the rules where confusion may, and often does, exist. There is a need to overcome any misunderstanding and inconsistencies in judgement. In addition, any confusion a competitor or spectator may have concerning the awarding of penalties at a particular obstacle may be dispelled.

Fence Judges are also responsible for the safety of competitors and spectators at or near a fence. Any emergency must be dealt with effectively. The precautions and actions that need to be taken will be discussed fully.

It must be remembered that eventing is a sport. Rules are not written in tablets of stone and, while they need to be interpreted consistently, they should be applied with commonsense and fairness. Hardly an event goes by without some incident occurring which is unique in the Fence Judge's experience. On these occasions it is right to ask for the help of the Technical Delegate (FEI) or the BHS Steward. The rules do not provide for every eventuality and unforeseen or exceptional circumstances will need careful consideration. In these cases, it is the duty of the Ground Jury or the Steward to make a decision which is in as close a keeping with the intention of the Rules and General Regulations as possible. Any decision must be made in a sporting spirit.

An appreciation of this demanding sport comes from a greater understanding. This book aims to enable more Fence Judges, competitors and spectators to enjoy the cross-country phase of horse trials.

1 · IN THE BEGINNING: PRESENTED

Cross-country fence judging is both challenging and rewarding. There is far more to the pastime than the casual observer may be aware. So many events take place in spectacular surroundings or are set in the midst of beautiful, and often private, parkland. Of course, there are those days when the driving rain threatens to reduce score sheets to a saturated illegible mess, or a bitter east wind with its flurries of snow numbs feet and fingers to the very bone. This is character building! In contrast are the idyllic summer days when, perhaps beneath the shade of a splendid oak, it is a pleasure to eat lunch *al fresco*!

In addition, fences vary from event to event. Of course, there are always the old favourites but it is often interesting to note what use the course designer and builder has made of any natural features such as quarries, banks, ditches and water. Clever use has even been made of old bomb craters! All of these, combined with the nature of the terrain, influence the type of course which is built. They vary from the open, galloping courses to those with demanding hilly country, or a combination of both.

Then there are the people you meet: spectators, owners, competitors, officials and the many volunteers in running the event. Whatever the level of competition, it is always of interest to watch competitors walking the course either on their own or with their 'team' of helpers. It is fascinating to observe the careful study made of the obstacle, the checking of all angles of approach to determine the quickest and safest line, the pacing out of distances between the elements of a combination fence and the subsequent decisions made on the intended route to be taken. The plans of action can vary enormously. Sometimes a competitor will walk a line which had not occurred to the Fence Judge! On one such occasion, a competitor walking the course took a long and careful look at a possible track involving the alternative rails at the coffin fence. It was a most unusual and time-consuming route, twisting among the trees, but quite in order to approach the first element. Later on, with the competition well under way, a group of spectators loaded with picnic baskets positioned themselves to watch the fence in comfort − exactly on the line where that particular rider had walked and measured her approach. Although amazed that anyone would consider taking that route, when it was explained to them they moved immediately to another position where there was no danger of finding themselves in the path of an oncoming horse. A few horses later the very competitor in question came along and duly took the line through the fence which she had considered so carefully. No one else took it all day! The group of spectators, however, were most grateful and most impressed − and the Fence Judge relieved that the one particular rider had been observed earlier in the day. It always pays to take into account all lines of approach, however unlikely, that a competitor may take. So often there is one which is unique. Talking to spectators in between horses arriving to jump the fence is always a pleasure, whether it is to discuss or explain aspects of the obstacle, the way it is jumping, or the course in general.

Cross-country riding is all about the partnership between horse and rider. Event horses come in all shapes and sizes, but it is always a thrill to watch any fit horse jumping big, solid fences out of a galloping stride with courage and confidence and in perfect balance and harmony with the rider. Interesting, too, to watch the progress of novice horses and/or riders as they gain experience from one event to another. In a Three-Day Event the speed and endurance section calls for a horse which is well trained and has been brought to the peak of condition. Riders have to demonstrate their knowledge of pace as well as of their horse across country.

One of the main responsibilities of the Fence Judge is to judge and mark each competitor at the fence. Any faults which are committed and the penalties awarded are recorded on the Fence Judge's score sheets. These are collected regularly throughout the competition and taken to the Scorers who work feverishly to add up and check the scores of every competitor in order to

Figure 1. Presented.

obtain the final results.

One of the first lessons of judging that experience teaches is to decide whether a horse has been presented at the fence, i.e. has the rider directed the horse at the obstacle and instructed him to jump it? This is an important lesson since it is only while jumping or attempting to jump that judgements can be made and faults penalised. An exception to this involves the penalty zone surrounding fences at Three-Day Events. Having entered the zone, from whatever direction, competitors incur penalties for circling and for leaving it before attempting to jump the obstacle.[1]

A horse napping and wheeling half a field away is not presented and no penalties are given. This often comes as a surprise to those spectators who confuse the rules of showjumping with

[1] Penalty zone: Fédération Equestre Internationale (FEI), Article 536 Para. 1.

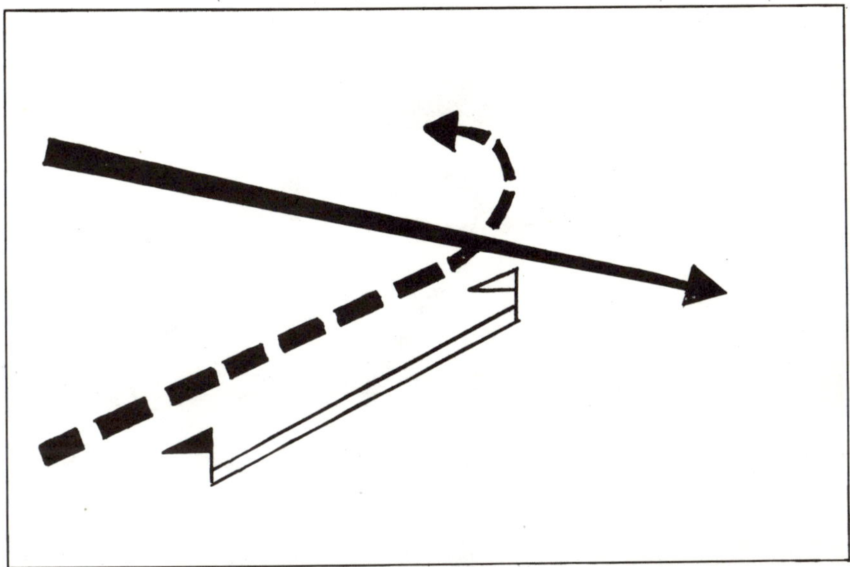

Figure 2. Single fence. Not initially presented: 0 penalties.

the rules for cross country. In showjumping any circle which causes the competitor to cross their tracks before jumping the next obstacle and any resistance, such as napping or going backwards, are penalised. On the cross-country course, however, riders are allowed to circle in between separately numbered fences before presenting at the next obstacle to be jumped. They may also dismount to adjust any part of the saddlery or to check the condition of the horse. No faults are committed. This also applies to riders who have 'lost' their way or who are out of control and gallop past the fence before returning to negotiate it (Figure 2). They are not initially presented and no penalties are awarded.[2]

Only precious time is lost as the time-keeper's clock continues to run. A competitor's time is recorded from the signal given to start until the horse's nose passes the finishing post. Time is counted in whole seconds with fractions rounded up to the next second and competitors are penalised 0.4 of a point for each second in excess of the optimum time set for the course. The optimum time is worked out according to the distance of the course and the speed set for a particular class. The speed for a Pre-Novice class is 490 m per minute, for example, and for an Advanced class 600 m per minute.[3]

[2] Definition of faults: British Horse Society (BHS), Rule 89.
[3] Distances and speeds: BHS, Rule 85.

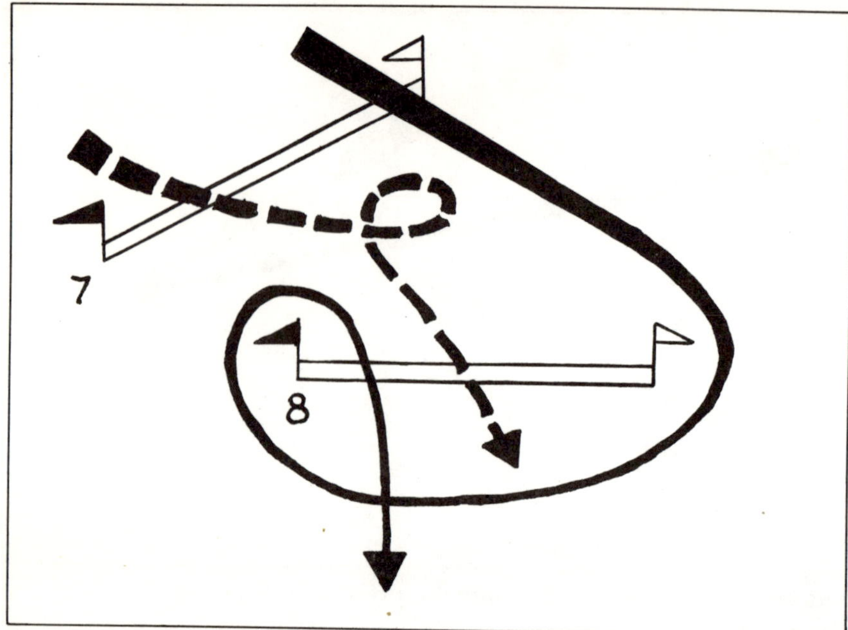

Figure 3. Adjacent fence. Not initially presented at fence 8: 0 penalties.

Although they are sited closely together, adjacent fences are numbered and judged as separate tests. Riders who do not initially present at the second fence cannot be penalised for run-outs or crossed tracks (Figure 3).

The rules are slightly different for a combination fence. Although consisting of separately lettered elements it is numbered and judged as one fence. Presentation at the first element means that a competitor is presenting at the whole complex. If the adjacent fences shown in Figure 3 become the two elements of a singly numbered fence as in Figure 4, the tracks taken by the rider are now penalised.

Judging only requires common sense and attention. Careful observation of the approaching combination of horse and rider enables the attitude of the horse and the intention of the rider to be assessed. This is important as some riders are capable of thinking fast on their horse's feet. One competitor, for example, made his approach and was committed to jumping the fence. In the last couple of strides the horse decided not to jump and planted his forefeet firmly into the base of the obstacle. Just remaining in the saddle and pausing for only a moment, the

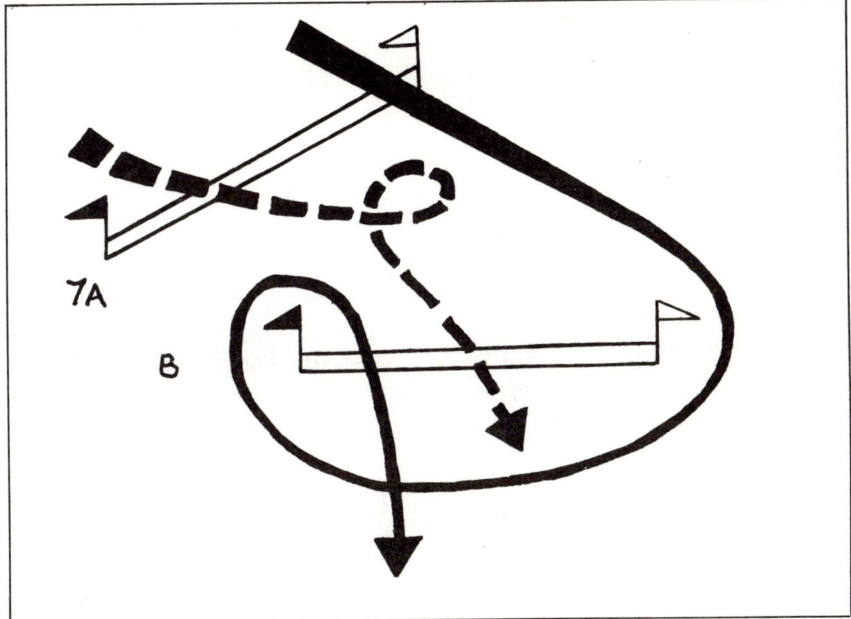

Figure 4. Combination fence. Presented at second element: 20 penalties for crossed tracks.

rider turned for the easier alternative rails set at a right angle to the direct route, calling out, 'I am not presenting!' Ten out of ten for initiative but 20 penalties for 'first refusal'.

The siting of some fences can be a judge's nightmare when deciding whether a horse is presented or not.

CASE STUDY 1

Competition: *Novice One-Day Event*

Fence: *Water complex consisting of three elements: (A) step down to a second step down into water (B) with a step up out of the water (C).*

The complex, built just below and out beyond the crest of the hill, meant that horses were able to catch sight of the water beyond as they came up the slope long before the first two elements were visible. At this point very novice, inexperienced horses in particular started baulking and refusing to go on. The problem was accentuated by the fact that they were coming away from 'home', i.e. the horse-box park. Were they presented?

Judgement: Some 30 or so yards away the combination could not be said to be presented. The rider may be trying to persuade the horse to go forward in the general direction of the fence but can hardly be said to be directing the horse at the fence with instructions to jump it. In this particular case one horse and rider at the foot of the slope leading up to the complex were finally eliminated as they were over the time allowed for the course. (This is twice the optimum time set for the course.)

The trouble in these situations is that the horse often makes a little progress forward before resisting again. A Fence Judge has to decide when the real commitment is made and the horse can be regarded as presented.

In a Three-Day Event, however, the penalty zone which extends 10 metres in front of an obstacle makes life easier for the Fence Judge. Any resistance made by the horse before crossing that line, i.e. outside the penalty zone, is not penalised. This may give some sort of guidance. On courses where penalty zones are not in existence, however, some fences may be sited in such a way that it would be difficult to 'measure' 10 metres and the commitment to the fence may be made much sooner.

CASE STUDY 2

Competition: *Novice One-Day Event*
Fence: *Drop into water*
The only approach competitors could take to the fence was down a narrow sloping pathway, hemmed in tightly on either side with banks covered by thick, impenetrable shrubs. The water lay straight ahead. It was very easy for competitors jumping the previous fence to over-run the narrow 'entrance' between the banks before they could make the very sharp turn into it.

Judgement: Not presented initially, they were not penalised. However, once a horse had come between the banks then the very nature of the track meant that the rider was committed to the obstacle ahead. They were now presented and were penalised for any faults incurred.

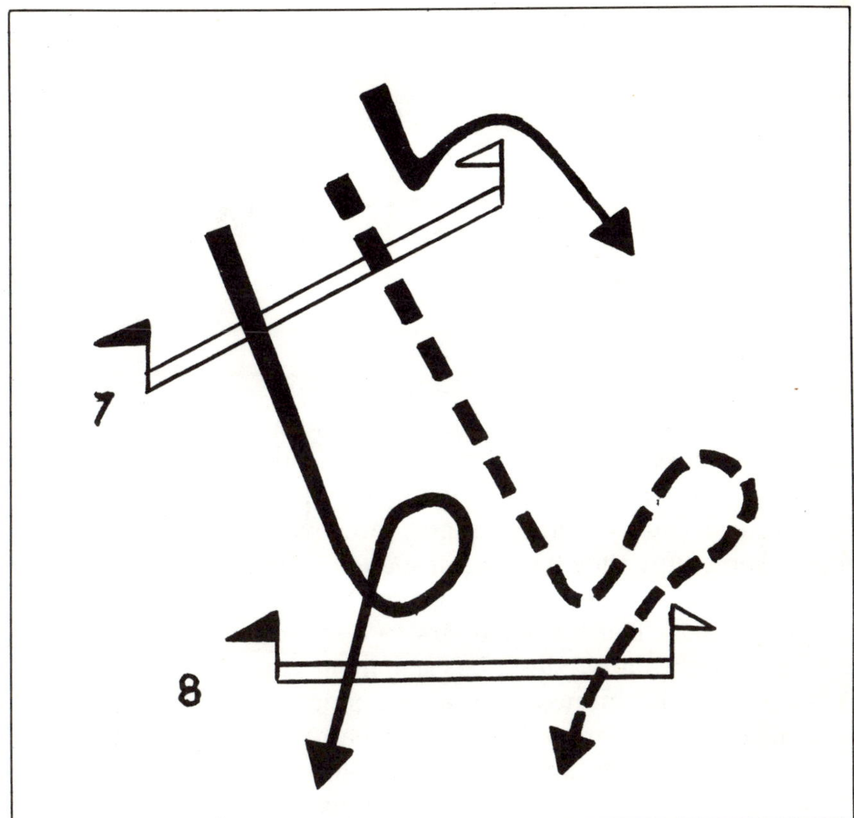

Figure 5. Presented: 20 penalties for a crossed track and run-out.

There are no magical measurements which can be made. It is entirely up to the Fence Judge to decide when a rider has directed the horse at the obstacle and asks him to jump it. It is a matter of understanding clearly the intention of the rider and the moment of commitment. Above all, it is important to be consistent.

Whatever the type of fence, once, in the judge's opinion, a rider has presented, judgement begins and penalties can be incurred.

2 · THE TROUBLE WITH REFUSALS

Obvious refusals are easy to judge — it is the moment the horse says 'No', stops in front of the fence and the rider has to turn away for a second attempt. Twenty penalties are incurred for a first refusal. Many Fence Judges, however, will acknowledge that at some time they have agonised over the words 'immediate' and 'prolonged' used in the British Horse Society Rules for Official Trials.[1] The former refers to a standing jump following a stop and the latter describes a halt in front of the obstacle. A horse jumping immediately after a stop is not penalised for a refusal. However, immediate does mean immediate in this case — the horse jumps straight away. Stop — one reminder with the whip — jump. This is immediate. However, stop — whack — no jump — whip applied again, is not an immediate jump. It is helpful to recall those competitors who jumped clear. This is a useful yardstick to dispel any lingering doubts as to whether the jump was immediate or not.

The term 'prolonged halt' can be misleading. Implicit in the phrase is the passage of time and novices could be forgiven for counting seconds. Many do so. Clearly the term describes what happens after a stop which is not followed by an immediate jump.

A prolonged halt is a favourite at open ditches and drop fences, particularly into water. The horse's technique may mean that he approaches and lowers himself very carefully. It can be agonisingly slow. This is fine as long as forward movement is maintained. A horse is also allowed to take one, maybe two, steps sideways before jumping but this does not imply that competitors may indulge in FEI dressage manoeuvres! A full pass along the entire length of the water's edge is not an immediate jump.

[1] Refusal: FEI, Article 538 Para. 1.1. BHS, Rule 89(a).

Figure 6. If the halt is prolonged ...

A step back, whether it is voluntary or not, even a single pace with any one foot, is decisive — it is a refusal. A horse 'paddling' up a sloping palisade can be regarded initially as forward movement and no problem if the horse, albeit with some difficulty, clears the obstacle. A judge, however, needs to be alert for the forelegs returning to the ground — a step back and certainly not an immediate jump. In a similar fashion, a horse can hesitate at a log into water, putting one or even both forelegs partly over the log before snatching them back again. This backward movement means it is a refusal. It is very important for the Fence Judge to be in the best position to see any foot going back.

The trouble is that riders so often do not turn away to re-present after one refusal. The rider is now very likely either to change or to intensify his efforts. Applying the whip instead of just using leg aids, or passing the whip into the other hand to apply to the other side of the horse, are examples of changes in effort. Applying legs and whip more strongly than before is an intensification of effort. Unless immediate success is achieved, a further fault is incurred — an additional 40 penalties for a second refusal.[2]

2 Refusal: FEI, Article 538 Para. 1.2. BHS, Rule 89(a).

Figure 7. Re-applied effort — by the rider.

It can all happen so quickly. A Fence Judge needs to watch carefully for renewed application of leg and whip by the rider as well as vocal encouragement, and for any backward movement by the horse. In the heat and drama of the moment riders are not always aware of what their horse's feet are doing. A horse, having stepped back, may then go forward immediately as the rider maintains his efforts with hand and leg, before taking another step back. This is a second refusal. Two, even three refusals, may be incurred very quickly. For this reason it is vital that refusals are called out clearly, leaving competitors in no doubt about the situation. If first and second refusals are not made clear it can come as a most unpleasant surprise when the competitor is told they are now eliminated for a third one. They may well challenge the judge by asking exactly where they received the other two refusals. It is thus very important to record clearly in the remarks column of the score sheet the details of what happened, in case of any future discussion concerning the incident: e.g. step back with near fore at element B. Certainly it is no good relying on memory alone. Several horses and incidents later will mean that it will be impossible to recall accurately what exactly took place to incur penalties.

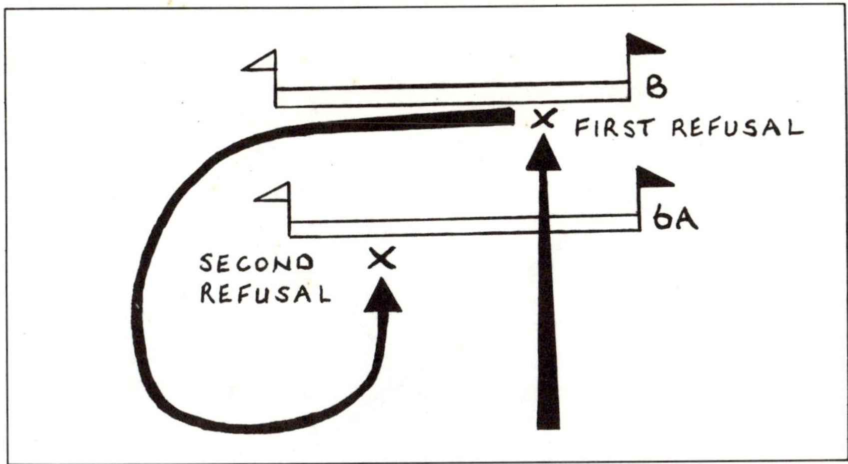

Figure 8. Combination fence: 60 penalties for two refusals.

After a refusal at an element of a combination fence a rider may elect to retake an element already jumped in order to present for a second attempt at the element where penalties were incurred. For example, a competitor jumps A but refuses at B. The rider then retakes A in order to approach and jump B. This is not an 'error of course' − a competitor is allowed to do this if they so wish with elements of a combination fence. However, if the horse now has a stop at A, even though he has cleared it once already, it is a second refusal, incurring 60 penalties in all (Figure 8; 20 for a first stop at B, and an additional 40 for a second stop when retaking A).[3]

Above all, judging must be consistent and the rules applied equally to every competitor. If, for example, a judge feels that after several horses have been through the fence, the judgements made concerning refusals have been somewhat lenient, or in contrast, rather harsh, then judgement must remain harsh or lenient for the rest of the competition. There is a case, perhaps, for being a little more generous on the third hesitation at an obstacle with horses competing at the lowest level of competition, i.e. Pre-Novice classes. These are young, inexperienced horses just setting out on their eventing career. Having been penalised for two stops at the same fence they are not going to win or be placed in the competition. It can be argued that it is more helpful to their future in the competitive scene if they are able

---

[3] Obstacle composed of several elements: FEI, Article 538 Para. 5.
  Faults at combination fences: BHS, Rule 89(e).

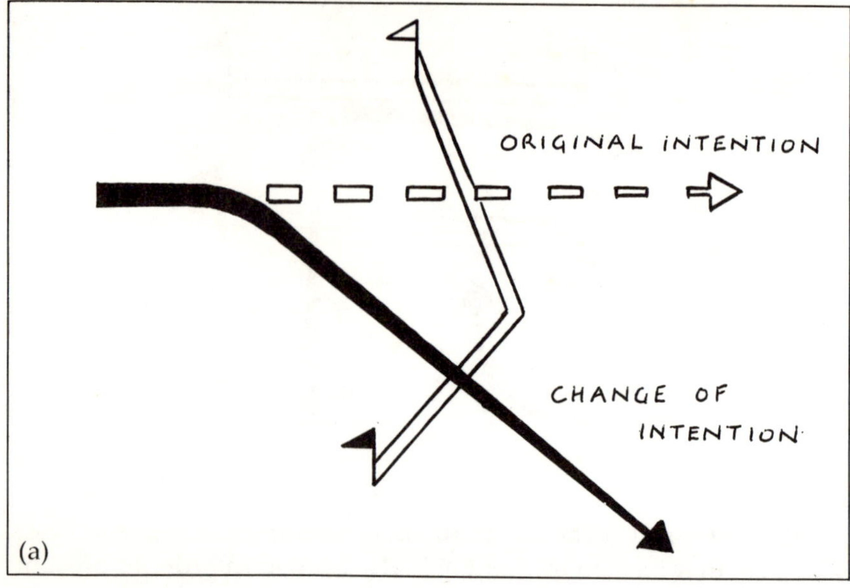

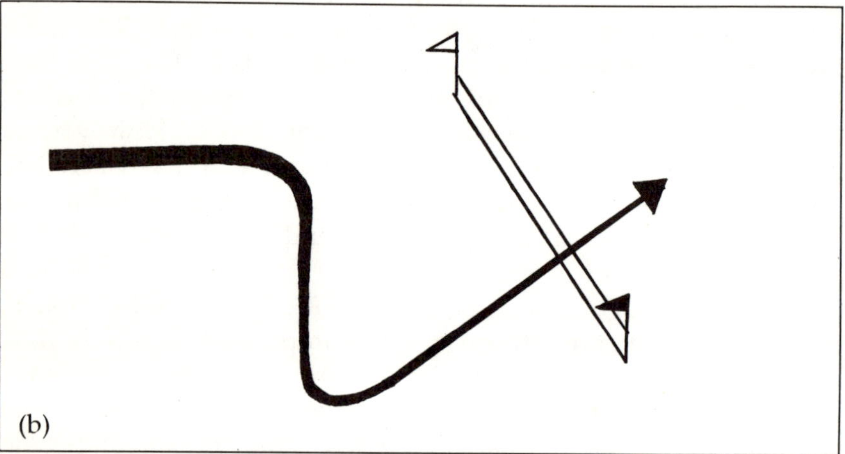

Figure 9. Change of rider's intention (and if not regarded as a refusal): 0 penalties.

finally to clear the obstacle posing the problem and so go on to finish the course. This does not, however, mean to suggest that the cross-country phase may be treated as a schooling session while the competition is in progress, or that any step back is disregarded or that prolonged halts may go on indefinitely. Care must also be taken to ensure that a following competitor is not impeded in any way.

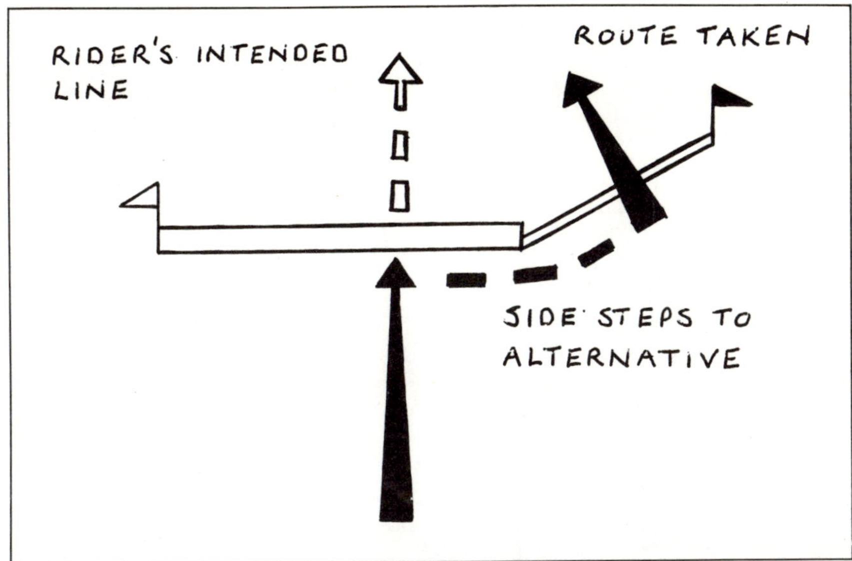

Figure 10. Rider's intention to jump the direct route: 20 penalties.

It is also important for a Fence Judge to assess carefully the intention of the rider. There are situations when a rider may change his mind after presenting without incurring penalties. The rider may feel that the horse is on a completely wrong stride or is too forward bound for safety and not really concentrating or responding to the rider's instructions. Changing to another line through the fence gives a little more time to re-establish balance and control and get the act together. It may be also that a competitor finds that he is not on the line he intended to take after walking the course, or it may be that he just changes his mind at the last moment. If the intention of the rider is clear and it is not the horse which is deciding the matter by trying to refuse or run out, then no penalties should be awarded (Figure 9).

A judge needs to be aware of the intention of the rider and the attitude of the horse. Is the horse going happily into the fence with eyes and ears alert, or are the ears laid flat back and is the whole manner of the horse one of reluctance? Is the rider intending to take the direct line through the fence? At a drop into water, for example, a horse stepping sideways and then dropping down to the lower alternative involving a change of direction is a refusal (Figure 10). The rider intended to jump the harder, direct route.

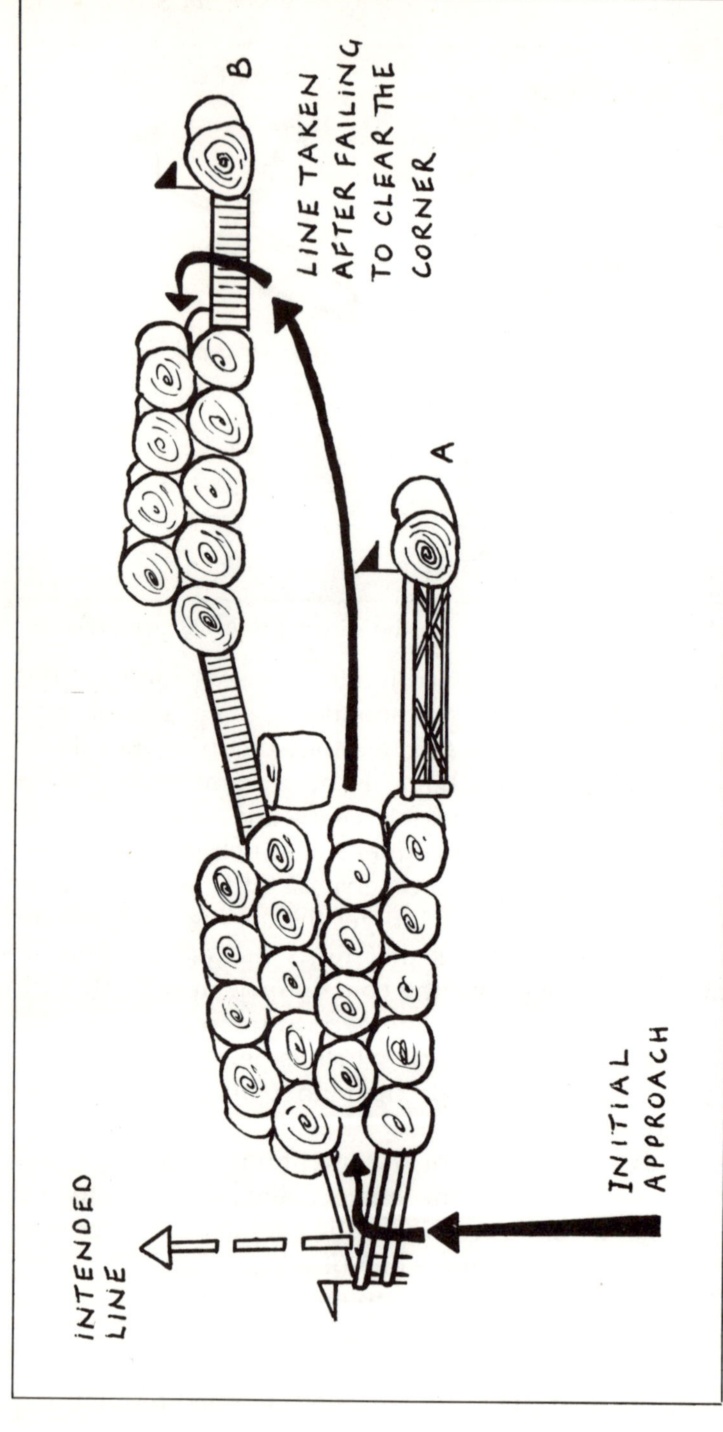

Figure 11. Rider's intention to jump A and B at the corner in one jumping effort: 20 penalties for a refusal at B.

CASE STUDY 3

Competition: *Intermediate One-Day Event*
Fence: *Combination consisting of two elements*
The quickest and most direct route entailed jumping a corner of rails which required accurate and bold riding. The fence was designed to make the longer, alternative route time consuming and a different approach was required in order to jump the two elements separately. In between the corner option and the alternative upright gate to a palisade were unjumpable walls of round straw bales (Figure 11).

As one competitor, fresh from the World Equestrian Games, rode for the corner, the horse faltered in the last two strides and tried to stop. However, the forward momentum carried his forelegs over the first rail leaving the horse straddled for a moment before he managed to scrabble the hind legs over. There was no option now but to take the longer route out over the second element.

Judgement: *20 penalties for a refusal. The intention of the rider was to clear the two parts of the obstacle with one jumping effort, i.e. over the corner. Failure to do so meant that it was a refusal at the second element even though the horse, somewhat untidily, managed to keep moving through the fence.*

All cross-country fences have the potential for a refusal from the very first obstacle to the last. Some fences, however, invite more refusals than others.

Water is always a challenge, particularly if it involves a drop into it. Horses have a natural reluctance to jump into water, and many young, inexperienced horses will give the Fence Judge good practice in calling out and recording refusals. Although water needs to be ridden at steadily, there does need to be enough impulsion so that a horse does not put in a stop. A Fence Judge, with experience, can often see when a refusal is imminent.

A coffin fence, with its three elements of post and rails on to a downhill slope to a ditch followed by an upward slope to a second set of post and rails, is a testing obstacle. So often horses do not concentrate on the first set of rails thus making them difficult to jump. They either concentrate on the ditch beyond or see it at the last moment and this frequently results in a refusal. In addition, a horse lacking enough impulsion may manage to clear the first two elements but not have enough, on uphill going, to clear the rails out. A coffin fence usually keeps a Fence Judge busy!

Steps up, like all uphill fences, need plenty of impulsion. The horse has to make several jumping efforts and a horse running out of steam can refuse at the top step because he is unable to cope with it. Fences situated on the edge of a wood mean that the horse is approaching out of light and jumping into deep shade. A refusal can occur because the outline of the fence will not be very clear to the horse. Refusals are sometimes caused by a wrong approach. Perhaps it is too slow with not enough impulsion to clear the obstacle, particularly when the going is soft and deep. Perhaps the rider is unable to keep the horse straight at the fence.

A Fence Judge, through experience, recognises the situations which can give rise to refusals and can often tell when a potential refusal is likely and so be prepared. Sometimes riders walk back after they have finished the course to discuss what caused the refusal and this is an added interest to the job. However, it is important that a Fence Judge does not enter into any discussion of faults or penalties with competitors who are challenging the refusal. They are certainly not allowed to come down and argue with you and if they do they must be referred immediately to the Steward or the Technical Delegate.

Whatever the reasons for a stop on the cross-country course three refusals at one obstacle, entailing elimination, can be clocked up all too soon.

3 · RUN-OUTS AND CIRCLES

Run-outs and circles incur the same scale of penalties as refusals and also count towards elimination.

Run-outs are usually obvious; the horse avoids jumping the obstacle by ducking out to either side of it.[1] The rider has to come back for a second attempt and incurs 20 penalties. Less obvious are run-outs involved when jumping close to one of the fence flags. Each fence has boundary flags positioned on either side of it which define the limits of the obstacle: a white flag on the left and a red one on the right. No penalties are awarded for knocking a flag down. However, if the horse's head passes on the wrong side — that is the outside — of the flag while he is negotiating the fence, it is penalised as a run-out. The competitor must re-take the obstacle. Failure to do so means they are eliminated for missing the fence which is an 'error of course'.[2] Competitors are allowed to ask whether they need to retake the obstacle and the Fence Judge must inform them. This is not regarded as outside assistance.

A corner fence, which requires both accurate and bold riding, is a good example of an obstacle where this sort of problem may arise. The best position for a Fence Judge is opposite the apex of the corner so that the flag is clearly seen and it is much easier to observe whether the horse's head has passed inside or outside of it. It can all happen so very quickly and a judge needs to pay particular attention in these cases and to be quite sure whether the competitors have, or have not, jumped the fence.

It is not considered a run-out if the horse avoids one part of the obstacle or an element and successfully jumps another part

[1] Run-out: FEI, Article 538 Para. 2. BHS, Rule 89(b).
[2] Errors of course: FEI, Article 533 Para. 3. BHS, Rule 75.

Figure 12. If the horse's head passes outside a fence flag, it is a run-out.

of the same obstacle or element. A horse coming in straight towards a fence initially and then taking a couple of strides at an angle before clearing the fence is not penalised as long as the deviation is not regarded as a refusal. The rider's intention was to take a certain line over the fence, the horse attempted to avoid doing so but the rider was able to keep the horse going forward to clear the obstacle at a different point along it. This is not the same as the horse avoiding jumping the more difficult option and changing direction to take an easier one.[3]

Circles are more complex. Once presented, if the horse crosses its original track with all four feet, it has circled (for this reason this disobedience is also referred to as cross tracks).[4] A Fence Judge needs to watch the track taken by a competitor very

[3] Definition of faults: FEI, Article 538 Para. 2.
[4] Circle: FEI, Article 538 Para. 3.1. BHS, Rule 89(c).

closely. One, two, or even three feet over the incoming track is not a 'circle' and if there is any doubt whatsoever concerning the fourth foot then the benefit must always be given to the rider. The routes taken through a fence by competitors can be most inventive and most demanding on the Fence Judge's powers of observation. 'Circles' in water can be more tricky, but commonsense will always cope with these situations.

The question of whether a horse has been presented or not, however, is paramount. A competitor, having jumped the previous fence, may decide to circle before asking the horse to go on and jump the next fence. This is often the case when a rider wishes to gain control and balance with a headstrong horse before tackling a difficult obstacle. Or it may be that the soundness of the horse is suspect and needs to be assessed before continuing or that some part of the equipment needs adjusting. Whatever the reason, no penalties are awarded because the combination have not yet presented at the next obstacle. This often confuses those spectators who assume that the cross-country rules are the same as those for showjumping, where a competitor is penalised for any circle between fences during the round.

It has also been known for riders, finding that the horse is on a totally wrong stride or far too headstrong and not 'listening' to the rider's instructions, to pull out deliberately at the last moment in the interests of safety. Again the intention of the rider is usually quite clear and this is not regarded as a run-out. A Fence Judge, however, must observe whether it is the horse dictating the action or whether it is the rider who is in total control. The difference between the two is 20 penalties. If they have not been penalised for a run-out, the combination must, however, be very careful not to cross their original track in returning to jump the obstacle because they were initially committed to it (Figure 13).

In the same way, circles between closely sited, adjacent fences may only be made without incurring penalties if the competitor does not initially present at the second fence or if penalty zones are not involved (Figure 14). The Fence Judge must watch the attitude of the horse and the intention of the rider.

The rules change for combination fences. Having presented at the first element, competitors may not circle between elements or go round an element to make the approach to the next one

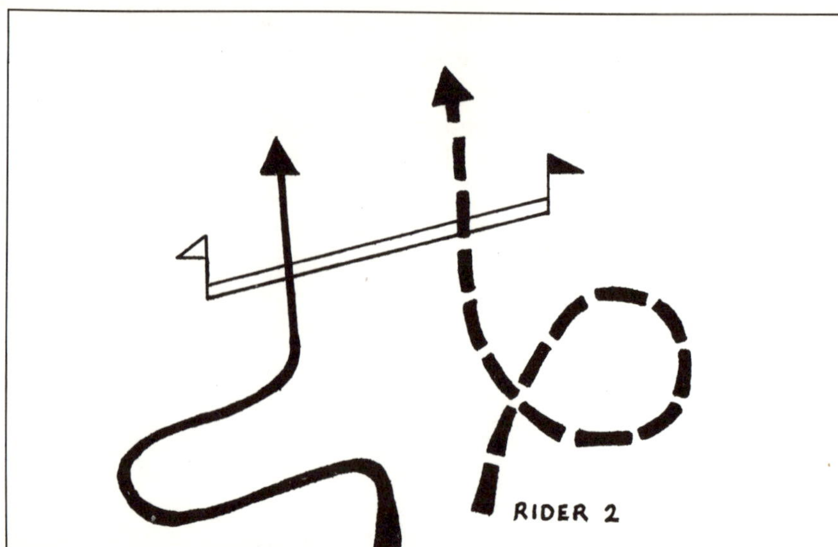

Figure 13. Single fence. Both riders are presented but their intention is clear to pull out. No penalties are awarded for a run-out although rider 2 receives 20 penalties for crossing the incoming track.

easier. If the adjacent fences in Figure 14 now become the two lettered elements of a single fence (i.e. 6A and 6B), faults are incurred each time: for deviating round an element to make the approach to the next one easier, and for crossed tracks.

Some riders will deliberately angle the first element of a combination fence and pull out to the side before coming back to jump the next. This is sometimes done to give the horse, particularly a young, inexperienced one, more time to cope with the different parts of the obstacle. It is, of course, time consuming but quite in order − as long as the original track is not crossed. Angles and distances are always painstakingly paced out by riders while walking the course and, quite often, specific landmarks are chosen to get angles and turns accurate. However, the best-laid plans all too often go wrong in practice! Jumping far faster and deeper than anticipated, some end up floundering in the chosen landmark. On one such occasion a competitor, carefully extracting horse and self from the midst of a very large rhododendron with as much dignity as they could

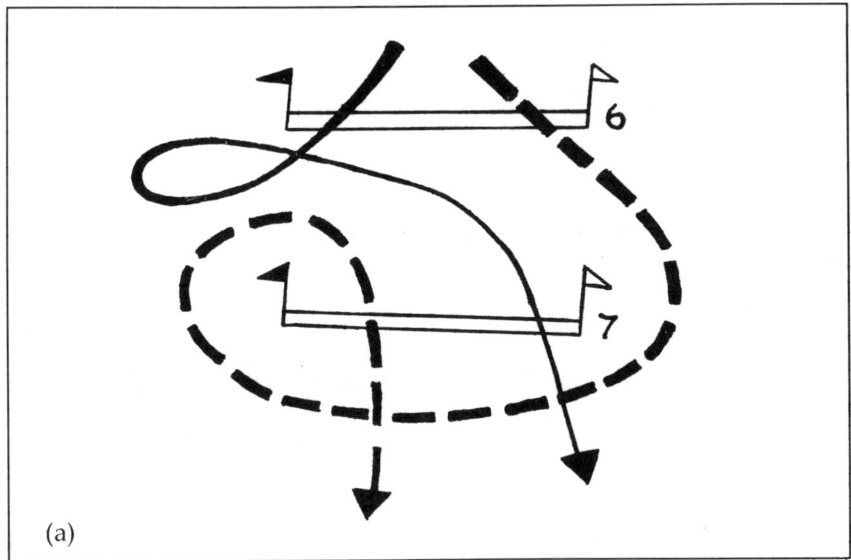

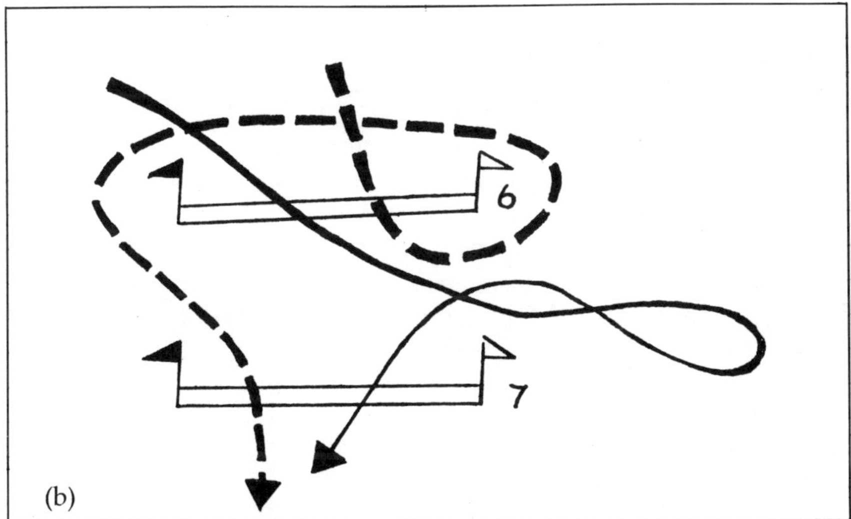

Figure 14. Adjacent fences. Not presented at fence 7: 0 penalties; but if these become a combination fence, faults are incurred each time.

muster in such a situation, commented, 'I really can't understand this. I'm sure there was more room when I walked it this morning — I don't suppose the bush has been moved?' Very difficult in such cases, if not impossible, if there is little space in which to manoeuvre, to avoid crossing tracks.

Competitors do not always understand, in the heat of the competition, how they can possibly have crossed their tracks. Certainly if a rider turns away on the 'wrong' rein then it will be inevitable that somewhere along the line they will cross their incoming track; for example, pulling out to the left and continuing to take a left rein back round to the fence. One such rider in a novice class did exactly this while holding a dialogue with the Fence Judge. Having made it quite clear, verbally, that she thought that the horse was all wrong in the last few strides, she pulled out hard to the left.

> *Competitor*: Am I all right? You know I pulled out on purpose, don't you? (All this said as she struggles to regain control and balance the horse.)
> *Judge*: Not a run-out! No penalties!
> (The competitor continues round at the trot on the left rein to jump the fence.)
> *Competitor*: Am I still all right?
> *Judge*: Yes...You are still all right.
> *Competitor*: Still OK?
> *Judge*: No...you have just crossed your tracks.

In this case the rider laughed, said she thought she would at some point, and then went on to jump the fence. This was an interesting and somewhat amusing incident. If the competitor had been told that they were inevitably going to cross their line then it would have been possible for them to have changed rein and taken another line to avoid penalty − there was just enough room to do so. This would have been forbidden, outside assistance − by the Fence Judge! However, as in the case of the competitor landing in the rhododendron, although a rider may turn on the 'correct' rein to avoid crossing tracks, they have run out of space to avoid it.

CASE STUDY 4

Competition: *Intermediate One-Day Event*
Fence: *Combination of a rail above a dry stone wall followed by upright rails with a corner option.*
Built in a copse of mature beeches and shrubs so that competitors approached out of full daylight and jumped into deep shade. Taking the longer route through the fence involved a tight turn after jumping

element A in order to jump B. The rider jumped in too fast, could not possibly make the turn, and ploughing through the shrubbery, passed dangerously close to one of the trees. Collecting his horse back together he then carefully took the 'correct' rein in an attempt to avoid crossing his track. However, the trees meant that there was no room left to avoid this in making a suitable approach to element B. The incoming track was crossed with all four feet (Figure 15).

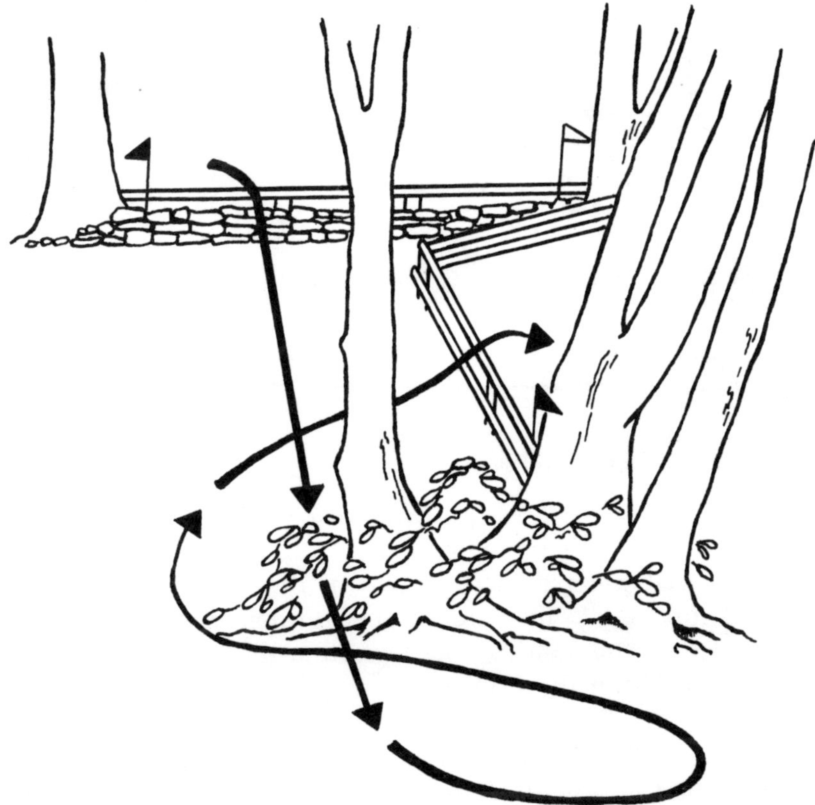

Figure 15. Combination fence. After overshooting the second part, the rider has run out of space and cannot avoid crossing tracks in order to make a new approach.

Judgement: 20 penalties for crossing tracks upheld after an objection by the rider to the awarding of penalties. A clear plan had been drawn on the score sheet at the time of the incident and after the line taken by the competitor had been carefully walked by the Fence Judges.

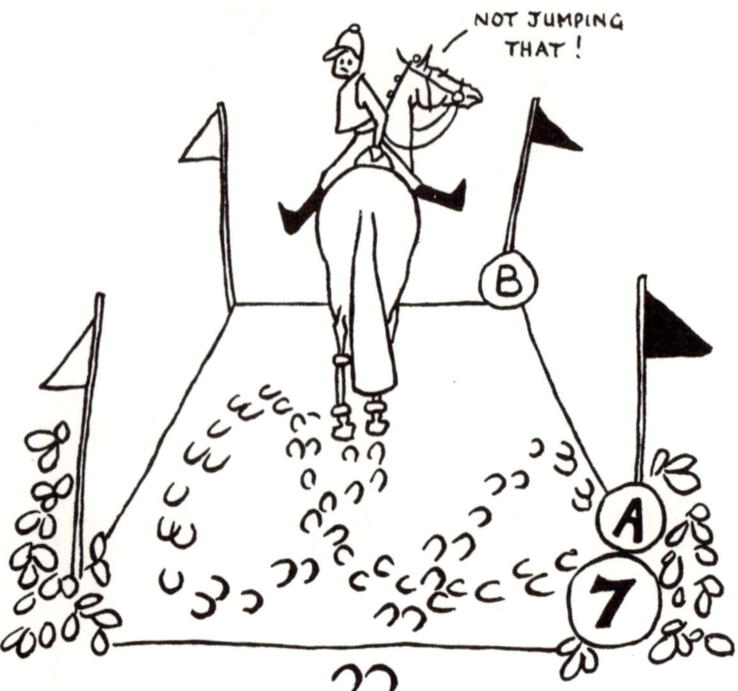

Figure 16. Second 'refusal'?

It is vital that diagrams are drawn at the time to show what exactly happened to incur faults. In addition it is a very useful back-up to ask the co-judge or steward at the fence to agree the track taken. Often the hoof prints will be clearly visible which makes drawing the diagram easier. A useful hint here: if the ground is soft and the fence is one which is likely to lend itself to crossed-tracks situations, then the marks left by one competitor need to be trodden in, making the next set of tracks easier to see. This will prevent any confusion!

It is easier to judge crossed tracks before a fence when there is a penalty zone (at Three-Day Events), and this will be discussed in the chapter concerning penalty zones.

Penalties are cumulative. A circle between elements of a combination fence, for example, followed by a refusal means 60 penalties. Whatever the type of fence, after a penalty has been awarded, a rider may circle freely without incurring further faults before re-presenting.

4 · THE BIG 'E': ELIMINATION

On the cross-country course, competitors are eliminated after a third refusal, run-out or circle at the same fence. The Fence Judge informs them clearly that they are eliminated and records it on the score sheet — a big 'E'.

At a Three-Day Event there is a new addition to the awarding of penalties on the cross-country phase (phase D) of the speed and endurance test. A competitor is eliminated for the fifth refusal, run-out or circle on phase D.[1]

Once eliminated at a fence, competitors may take no further part in the competition and they are reminded by the Fence Judge that they must leave the course at a walk[2] — it can be a long and lonely one. No further obstacles may be attempted despite anguished pleas of 'It's his first event — can't we have just one more go?' In addition, the horse must not be abused in any way. Whether elimination occurred at their fence or not, Fence Judges must report any transgression such as digging the horse with the spurs, striking him with the whip, or jobbing him in the mouth. Any behaviour like this is recorded on the judge's score sheet and the wrath of the BHS Steward awaits those competitors on their return.

At one Intermediate event, a rider who had been eliminated elected to take the horse through the water by an easy unflagged route before leaving the course. This was an understandable action as the rider at least managed to persuade the horse into the water and because there was no other competitor approaching the fence there was no danger of another rider being impeded. However, once the horse was in the water the rider laid into

---

[1] FEI Bulletin No. 12, 1992 (an addition to Article 537 Para. 1.1).
[2] After elimination: FEI, Article 533 Para. 9. BHS, Rule 81.

him with the whip — a senseless and useless action. The horse entered the water, which was the purpose of the exercise, and got beaten for it. The Technical Delegate happened to be passing at that very moment and his fury resounded round the course. The incident was recorded against the competitor's number. In any case involving the abuse of a horse, a report is required and, where possible, a statement taken from one or more witnesses.

There is some concern about situations where crossed tracks, which is regarded as a technical refusal, count towards elimination. A fair attitude, expressed by some, is that the competitor is not verbally eliminated by the Fence Judge but allowed to continue. If the rider subsequently makes an objection to the penalty awarded for crossing tracks, and the objection is upheld, it means that the competitor can be scored because they were not prevented from finishing the course. Sometimes it may be difficult to let a competitor know they are eliminated. A competitor having two refusals at element A of a combination fence, for example, may clear it at the third attempt but then cross their tracks before jumping out over element B. By the time the Fence Judge has taken a breath to call it out, horse and rider may be vanishing fast into the far distance. It can only be recorded on the score sheet.

Elimination can be incurred for other reasons. These are not enforced by the Fence Judge, but their documented observations are vital. Each case is decided by the BHS Steward or the Technical Delegate. Under the heading of 'forbidden assistance' the rules are clear: no intervention by a third party intended to help the competitor is allowed, whether it is asked for or not.[3] This is easy to apply if friends or relatives of a competitor suddenly leap out of the bushes at the appropriate moment brandishing lunge-reins or a yard broom.

Friends are not allowed to be posted at certain points on the course to call out directions or to make signals as the competitor passes by. It is also strictly forbidden for anyone (except event officials) to use any kind of receiving apparatus. Competitors may not be accompanied, followed or preceded anywhere on the course by anyone on foot, mounted on horseback or bicycle, or in a vehicle. Under the same rule, no one is allowed to interfere in any way with the fences or any part of the course — moving flags or markers, for example, or breaking off branches.

[3] Unauthorised assistance: FEI, Article 533 Para. 8. BHS, Rule 80.

Figure 17. Outside assistance at the fence.

More difficult to deal with are interventions by spectators who are unaware of the rule. At a Novice event, a competitor suddenly found they were momentarily 'lost' and asked where the next fence was. 'Down there, luv, on the left', the spectator replied. In this instance, it was not crucial. Wrongly directed, the competitor returned moments later as she realised that there was another fence to be jumped first. A few quiet words in the spectator's ear ensured it was understood why such 'Only trying to be helpful' advice was not permitted. Likewise, any error of course must be rectified by the rider without any help from anybody else. Calls of 'You've missed out fence nine', is outside assistance. The only exception to this is when a fence flag is knocked down. Riders are allowed to ask the judge whether they need to retake the fence. Otherwise, any action to help the horse or rider to win or be placed in the competition is forbidden.

Crowds of spectators gathered round a fence pose different problems. An outburst of 'clicking' and other verbal encouragement can occur as a competitor comes in for a final attempt at the water. When challenged, a wall of innocent faces stares silently

Figure 18. Outside assistance on the course.

back. A Fence Judge imposes authority firmly but kindly, and trusts that further incidents are squashed. Anyone believed to have helped horse and rider must be identified and Fence Judges also need to take names of reliable witnesses — it could be crucial.

Every numbered and lettered fence on the cross-country course must be jumped in the correct order. Competitors must pass between all boundary flags, keeping red on the right and white on the left. Any error of course which is not corrected results in elimination. Fence Judges, regardless of whether it is their fence or not, must record the omission of an obstacle if they observe it. The judges at a fence tucked away in a wood may not be able to see enough of the course and be totally unaware that they have been by-passed. In one such situation, the judge on the fence in the wood walked down to the previous obstacle to enquire what the hold-up on the course was all about. There was no hold-up, but three riders in a row had missed his fence out!

Once a fence has been jumped in the wrong order the rider cannot go back and redeem the situation. A rider jumping fence five, for example, after jumping fence three cannot correct the mistake by going back to jump fence four.[4] After an incident at Badminton Three-Day Event in 1973 where a horse and rider

---

[4] Error of course: FEI, Article 533 Para. 3. BHS, Rule 75.

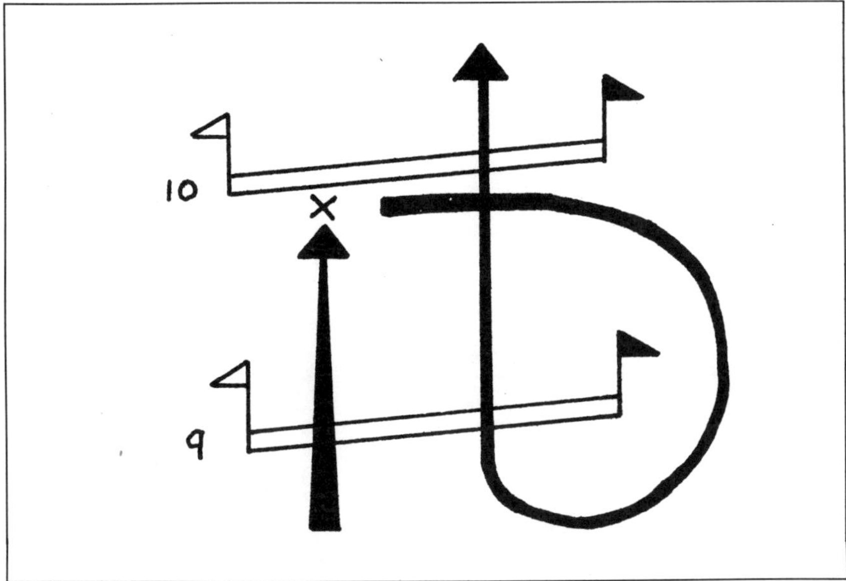

Figure 19a. Elimination for jumping a fence already taken after the refusal at fence 10.

scrambled under the log suspended over a deep ditch, it was ruled that competitors must go over fences. All reasonable precautions are now taken by course builders to prevent the possibility of a competitor being able to pass under an obstacle while still mounted.[5]

Retaking a fence already jumped also entails elimination. This can so easily happen when two separately numbered fences are sited close together, such as a ditch followed by post and rails, if the horse puts in a stop at the second fence. The rider may not come back round and retake the first fence in order to make an approach to the second one again. Neither may he recross the ditch the wrong way between the flags to have a second run at the second fence (Figure 19a).

The exception to this rule involves combination fences. A competitor, after a refusal or a fall at any part of the obstacle, may retake an element which has already been jumped if he wishes to do so. He does not have to. However, if he chooses to do so, he may also pass the wrong way between the flags in order to achieve this and does not incur any penalties (Figure 19b).[6]

---

[5] Nature of obstacles: FEI, Article 534 Para. 3.1. BHS, Rule 86(b).
[6] Obstacle composed of several elements: FEI, Article 538 Para. 5. BHS, Rule 89(e).

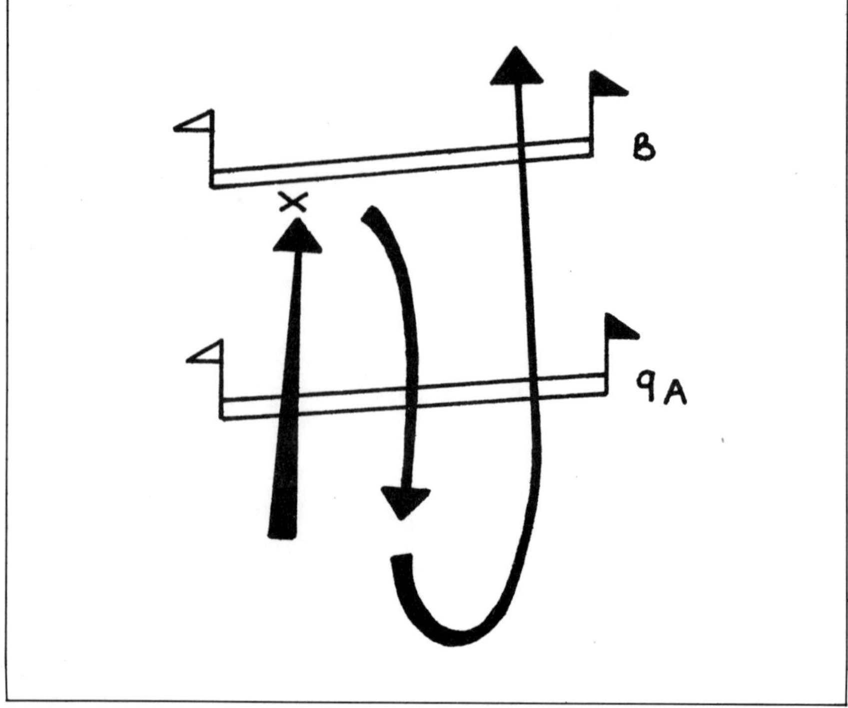

Figure 19b. 20 penalties only for the refusal at element B.

(The rules are slightly different to those of showjumping, where after a refusal or run-out in a combination fence a rider must retake the whole obstacle again or they will be eliminated.)

CASE STUDY 5

Competition: *Novice One-Day Event*

Fence: *Combination consisting of two sets of upright rails with alternative approaches to each element. The fence was situated towards the bottom of a fairly steep slope.*

The direct route was a straight line down the hillside from the previous fence, over element A, then three strides and out over B. The longer, time-consuming route involved taking a reversed 'S' line over the alternatives. Accurate riding was required for the direct line out over the second element because the rails were narrower than the first set of rails. In between the direct and alternative routes were wooden fence panels.

Two riders, during the competition, jumped in fast over the first element and rode straight over the fence panel adjacent to the white flag which marked the boundary of the rails at the second element. The first rider continued on and successfully negotiated the next, separately numbered fence, while the second rider returned immediately to jump element B (Figure 20).

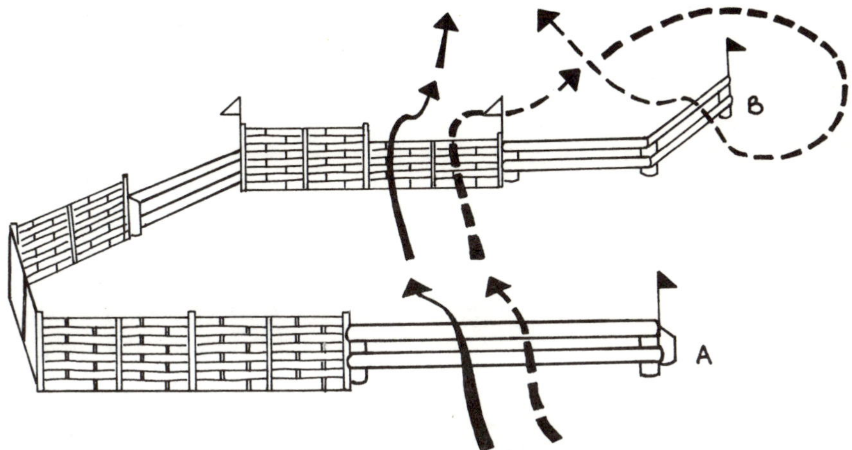

Figure 20. The first rider (solid line) is eliminated for an error of course which is not rectified. The second rider (dotted line) rectifies the error of course and only receives 20 penalties for a run-out or crossed tracks.

Judgement: The first rider is eliminated because, having jumped outside the fence flag, they continue on and jump the next fence. They have therefore omitted to jump element B — an error of course. The second rider corrects the error of course and is only penalised for crossing their tracks (it can be argued that the penalties could be awarded for a 'run-out' at the second element). Whatever reason is given, it all adds up to the same thing — 20 penalties.

Dangerous riding also carries the penalty of elimination.[7] The rules are explicit: in between obstacles a faster competitor catching up a slower rider in front may only overtake in a safe and proper manner and at a safe and suitable place. The slower rider must give way, but competitors have to work this out between themselves. Their verbal exchanges can be quite a revelation!

[7] Overtaking: FEI, Article 533 Para. 5.3. BHS, Rule 77.

Figure 21. Riders must only overtake at a safe and suitable place.

However, neither rider must deliberately obstruct or cause any
danger to the other.

It is important that Fence Judges make a note on their score sheet of any incident which infringes this rule. The matter will then receive the attention of the BHS Steward or the Technical Delegate.

In a similar way, and under the same rule as above, when the rider in front is committed to jumping an obstacle, it is dangerous riding if the following rider jumps that obstacle and interferes with or endangers the other.[8] A Fence Judge could only intervene when the leading horse has incurred a fault at the fence, before the new amendment of the rule, introduced in 1992, came in to force. In this situation the rider was then asked to stand to one side and allow the following competitor through. Under the new ruling a Fence Judge now has the power to order the slower rider to stand aside for the faster competitor coming up hard behind, even though they have not incurred any penalty at the fence. Failure to follow the instructions of the Fence Judge or any other Official means elimination at the discretion of the BHS Steward or the Ground Jury.[9] This is fair. The slower rider has probably had problems already on the course which is why they are about to be overtaken by the following competitor, who may well go on to win the competition!

There are, however, dangers here. First, the slower rider should only be waved aside as they make their approach and not when they are already committed to the obstacle. Secondly, even though Control may have warned the Fence Judge via radio that this sort of situation is developing and to be prepared to pull out the slower horse, there is no guarantee that the first competitor on the scene is in fact the slower one! They may have already changed their order and the numbers on riders' tabards are not always easy to read as they approach at speed. There is a real danger that the faster rider, now in front, is the one which is stopped. This is the very situation which no one wished for! For this reason, it may be wise to time the horse as it comes past the timing marker before signalling it to pull out. If the slower rider is stood aside, the time taken before they continue on course is not recorded. However, if the faster competitor is flagged down by mistake, at least their 'hold-up' time can be documented and they can be sent off smartly on their way with no real loss of rhythm.

In other situations it may be a question of safety.

---

[8] Overtaking: FEI, Article 533 Para. 5.2. BHS, Rule 77.
[9] Overtaking: FEI, Article 533 Para. 5.3. BHS, Rule 77.

CASE STUDY 6

Competition: *Novice One-Day Event*

Fence: *Combination of two elements of upright rails situated on the edge of dense woodland with a narrow track leading down to it. The fast route was over a corner, jumping both elements in one effort, while the longer option was set at right angles to the straight line through.*

It was apparent by the commentary over the public address system that an overtaking situation could be imminent. The first and obviously slower rider appeared and elected to take the longer option (no surprise), which meant a circular detour around a substantial clump of trees and shrubs after clearing the first element in order to jump the second. As they jumped A the faster following competitor appeared out of the trees and made their approach for the corner option. It was quite clear that this was suddenly a kami-kazi situation! The timing of both riders, taking alternative lines through the fence, meant a collision was inevitable (Figure 22). The Fence Judge at B signalled clearly to the first rider that they were to stop — even though they were between elements — and she did. The co-judge at A, unable to see whether the first competitor had responded because of the trees, stopped the faster competitor. The second rider's time was taken and, with no danger now, he was told to continue on. The 'hold up' only took some 20 seconds! In due course, the other rider was also sent on their way. Their hold-up time was, of course, not recorded. Although they now had to circle to make an approach to

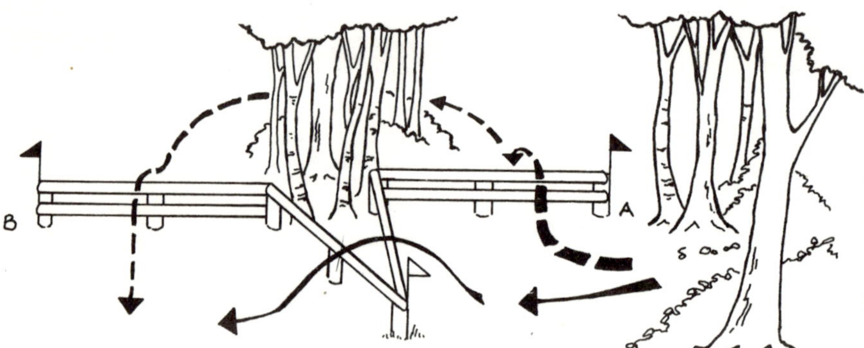

Figure 22. The slower rider (dotted line) elects to take the slower route. The faster rider (solid line) takes the direct route over the corner. The timing of both riders meant that a collision was inevitable unless one of them was stopped.

element B again, this was not counted against them. To be fair, they had responded to the request to stop in the middle of the fence, and a possible disaster had been avoided.

Certainly the slower rider had already experienced problems earlier on in the course which is why they were being overtaken, and they obviously would not be placed in the competition.

When a slower rider, or one who has problems at a fence, is asked to stand aside to let the following competitor through, they must be careful not to take a lead by following the other horse too closely. This is regarded as 'unauthorised assistance' and it incurs elimination.[10] Under the same rule, a competitor is not allowed intentionally to join another competitor and to continue the course in company with him.

As a postscript, the faster rider does not have divine right to overtake or verbally to intimidate the slower rider. Some believe they have, and do. Riders on slower horses, but making steady progress, can have their rhythm broken and then face the real threat of being accused of taking a lead. The Fence Judge does now have more control over the situation as a result of the new ruling. At least the slower horse which has already had problems can be cleared from the fence before it can impede or influence the following rider. Certainly with novice horses, if the horse in front stops, it is quite likely that the following horse will too!

Finally, the second fall of horse or rider on the cross-country course also results in elimination.

[10] Unauthorised assistance: FEI, Article 533 Para. 8. BHS, Rule 80.

5 · FALLS

Cross-country fences are fixed, solid obstacles. They do not give way easily when hit, and failure to clear them cleanly usually results in a fall of horse and/or rider. For any Fence Judge, falls probably represent one of the most testing incidents on the course. The situation needs to be assessed quickly and action taken calmly.

A rider is said to have 'fallen' when he becomes separated from his horse and has to remount.[1] Dismounting as a result of attempting to jump an obstacle, whether it is voluntary or not, is penalised as a fall. There have been incidents when the competitor has used the fence itself to prevent themselves from falling off after the horse has put in a sudden stop. The question to ask is, 'If the fence had not been there to enable the rider to push themselves back in the saddle, would they have fallen to the ground?' If the answer is a definite 'yes' then it should be penalised as a fall. The situation is, perhaps, a debatable one.

A horse is said to have 'fallen' when at the same time both its shoulder and hindquarters touch the ground or fence and the ground. A horse slipping and 'sitting down' before regaining its feet is not a fall. Sixty penalties are awarded for a fall of horse and/or rider.

These penalties are only awarded if the fall is connected with jumping or attempting to jump an obstacle. After a mistake at the fence, like hitting it very hard, a rider, now unbalanced, may manage to cling on for some distance before finally parting company with the horse. The eventual fall is directly connected to the manner in which the fence was jumped, and at One and

---

[1] Falls: FEI, Article 538 Para. 4. BHS, Rule 89(d).

Figure 23. Sixty penalties for a fall.

Two-Day Events it is penalised. A hopeful cry of 'I'm not falling off, I'm dismounting' means that the Fence Judge needs to pay close attention to detail. There is a difference of 60 penalties between the two situations.

Falls outside the penalty zone of a Three-Day Event are not penalised, even if the parting of horse and rider is the result of how the fence was jumped.[2] Determined riders have been known to cling on almost upside-down, while encouraging the horse to leave the zone, before finally giving in to the laws of gravity! A slip-up on the flat, unconnected with jumping, also incurs no faults. This type of fall, however, can be serious and Fence Judges need to be alert to the possibility that medical or veterinary attention may be required. If a rider dismounts between separately numbered fences to adjust any part of his own or the horse's equipment, or to pick up his riding whip, or whatever, this is not penalised as a fall. Competitors are also allowed to do this after incurring a fault at an obstacle before they present once more. Time is the only thing ticking away against them with the possibility of picking up penalties for exceeding the optimum time set for the course.

Many falls of the rider involve the horse putting in a sudden stop or swerving at the last moment to avoid the fence, and unseating the jockey. This incurs 60 penalties for a fall in addition to 20 penalties for a refusal — 80 penalties in total. This accumulation of penalties may also apply to the situation in

[2] Penalty zone: FEI, Article 536 Para. 5.

Figure 24. Eighty penalties.

which a horse becomes trapped on the fence and is liable to injure itself or cannot proceed without assistance. In order to extricate the horse and minimise any injury, the Fence Judge has the authority to order the rider to dismount. As soon as the rider's feet touch the ground it is penalised as a fall! Some fences may be low enough for the horse to scramble his well-greased hind legs over with the rider still in the saddle if they are given a moment, but as soon as this appears not to be the case, the rider must be instructed to dismount. If the horse and rider are judged not to have passed between the fence flags then the competitor is awarded an additional 20 penalties for a refusal.[3]

This rule is easy to apply to a spread fence where the horse is trapped on the first part of the obstacle, so there is no question of the complete fence being jumped. It is a far more testing situation when this happens at a straightforward upright fence, which calls upon keen observation and assessment by the Fence Judge.

[3] Competitors in difficulty: FEI, Article 533 Para. 6.2. BHS, Rule 78.

CASE STUDY 7

Competition: *Three-Day Event*
Fence: *Combination consisting of four elements composed of upright rails, the first three elements situated on a downhill slope.*
At the last moment the horse put in an extra, short stride before the first element which took him too deep into the fence. Unable to check the forward momentum, the horse put both forelegs over the top rail, throwing the rider out of the saddle at the same time to an eventual fall on the downhill landing side of the fence. With the horse straddled over the fence, the rider recovered quickly, picked up the reins and encouraged the horse to scramble out over the rails. The competitor then remounted and continued out over elements B, C and D.

Initial judgement: *The rider was awarded 60 penalties for a fall and 20 penalties for a first refusal. They were then eliminated for not retaking element A.*

Subsequent judgement: *Following discussions with the Sector Steward and the Technical Delegate it was agreed that the horse and rider had remained together as they went through the fence flags. This meant that it was not a refusal and the combination were not eliminated for failing to retake the fence. It was just 60 penalties for a fall and meant that they could go forward for the final show-jumping phase.*

There is, perhaps, some confusion here for Fence Judges. The BHS pamphlet *Instructions to Fence Judges* which is handed out to each judge at every briefing for One, Two and Three-Day Events clearly states that 80 penalties are awarded when a horse is trapped on a fence and the rider is instructed to dismount (a refusal and a fall). However, the full rules in the *BHS Horse Trials Handbook* (1992), which is identical on this point to the FEI 1992 regulations, suggests that there is another assessment to be made of the situation. The rules state that the rider must be 'mounted to pass all red and white boundary flags'[4] and that only if 'the competitor and horse have not passed between the flags'[5] can a refusal and a fall be awarded. How can this be

[4] Pace and dismounting: FEI, Article 533 Para. 4.2. BHS, Rule 76.
[5] Competitors in difficulty: FEI, Article 533 Para. 6.2. BHS, Rule 78.

interpreted? It appears that as long as the horse with the rider 'mounted' in the saddle passes between the flags, i.e. the front half of the horse, it is not a refusal. They have attempted to clear the obstacle and the horse has not stopped in front of the fence and its boundary flags. The fact that the hind legs have not managed to follow suit means that 60 penalties will be incurred if the horse cannot scramble them over and the rider has to dismount.

Under the old rules the third fall of a horse and rider combination on the cross-country course entailed elimination. In the new ruling (1992) a competitor is eliminated for the second fall.[6] This is usually the remit of Cross-Country Control who have an overall picture of what is happening on the course and who advise the judge of the situation if there is radio contact between the two. Otherwise, even though the Fence Judge may have been listening enthralled to the cross-country commentary over the public address system and 'knows' this is the second fall of the competitor, they do not eliminate them. This may only be done if both falls have been observed and there is no doubt about it. A judge may also ask a rider if they have had a fall previously on the course; they are usually quite honest about this, unless suffering from loss of memory − or worse! The new rule does make sense. Riders often appear to be quite all right after a fall, re-mount and continue on the course only to have problems further on and then run the possibility of interfering with the following competitor. Two falls would seem to be enough for anyone in one competition! With at least 120 penalties they are not going to be among the prize winners. The health and safety of both horse and rider come first. Similarly, under the same rule a rider is now eliminated for the second fall on the steeplechase phase at a Three-Day Event. There are, of course, certain fences which very often catch out the unwary. Two favourites are the coffin fence and drops into water. A competitor coming in too fast at the coffin may result in both horse and rider landing in the ditch if they make up too much ground over the first element. The ditch is often sited on a downhill approach and this may cause the horse to peck or stumble towards the ditch if he has jumped the rails untidily, so unseating the rider.

[6] Falls: FEI, Article 537 Para. 1.2.

Water is the fence which attracts spectators. It is also the one where competitors dread making a spectacle of themselves. It is the speed at which the fence is jumped which is crucial. The 'drag' of the water can be enough to check a galloping horse in its stride so that the horse is 'tripped up', and down he goes. Coming in too fast causes another problem. The horse may manage to keep his feet, but the spray which is kicked up may blur the horse's view and there may not be enough time for him to see the fence out of the water clearly. This can lead to a refusal and possibly a fall. Some inexperienced horses jump far too big into water. The impact can unbalance the horse so that the rider is thrown forward and may be unseated. Experience tells a Fence Judge when a fall is imminent, especially when the angle and speed of landing means that the horse will be stopped drastically by contact with the water. So often, when a horse jumps too big and round into water, the steepness on landing results in a fall.

Of course, all obstacles on the cross-country course have the potential for a fall. Upright fences which can look quite innocent need to be jumped cleanly at speed. A take-off too close to a fence on a downhill slope may mean a fall if the horse catches the top rail. At a drop fence it is the rider who usually falls, particularly if they have allowed themselves to get too far forward. Spread fences can cause an unpleasant fall if they are taken at an angle because the width is increased, and this is especially the case with parallel bars which are so unforgiving. Jumping from light into dark will mean the horse will not see the fence easily unless given time to adjust. Fences which have a 'top' to them which is not very high may cause the horse to 'duck' his head and also to hit the fence because he does not pick up his legs quite high enough.

Fence Judges are not asked to document the reasons for any fall! However, there is a satisfaction if some indication can be given when the owner or rider comes back later to ask what went wrong. In a serious fall, these sort of details may be of great importance.

After a fall, or if a competitor dismounts, he may be given help in catching his horse, adjusting his saddlery, and remounting. In addition, he may also be handed any part of his equipment either while he is dismounted or after he has remounted. This is not forbidden assistance.

Under a new rule introduced in 1993, Fence Judges are now requested to record on their score sheets UR for an unseated rider and HF for a horse fallen. This is to distinguish whether fences are causing riders to fall or horses. If a particular fence is taking horses out then it may be modified or altered in future.

When new score books are printed there will be two columns under the heading for falls, one headed UR and the other HF. Judges will record penalties in the appropriate column.

Whatever the reason — a wrong approach, not straight, coming in too fast, too slow, or lacking in impulsion — falls are a serious business. Expert attention will be required immediately where injury has been sustained. A Fence Judge must be prepared to put emergency action into force and to be concerned with the health and safety of horse, rider, spectators, and oncoming competitors.

6 · EMERGENCY ACTION

In the tough and risky sport of eventing, accidents are inevitable. One of the most important responsibilities of a cross-country Fence Judge is to decide when to put emergency action into operation. It is this 'aspect of the job' which is so often of great concern to Fence Judges, particularly those who are inexperienced.

Fence Judges are responsible for the health and safety of competitors and spectators at and around the fence. They have the authority to take any action, tempered with commonsense, to prevent an accident or injury to horse and rider. Within this remit they have authority to prevent a competitor continuing on the course. Fence Judges must not allow themselves to be intimidated by owners, spectators, or friends of the competitor, but to make sure the rider waits for expert attention. The doctor and the vet have the ultimate say in the matter. At a Three-Day Event, under the revised rules for 1993, a Fence Judge must record the length of time a competitor is held while waiting for examination by the doctor or for the vet to check the horse. The time is required in case they are allowed to continue. If the doctor or vet decides that the rider should not continue, this must be reported to Control. Only the Ground Jury may formally stop them. However, most competitors accept the advice and retire.

Following a fall, a prompt and intelligent diagnosis of the situation must be made. Often horse and rider are merely winded and, given a few moments to recover, can be re-united and allowed to continue. However, if there is any doubt about their health, professional help must be sought immediately via Control. Fence Judges are provided with flags for this purpose. A red flag waved above head height requests the doctor, a blue flag requests the vet. The waving of these flags must continue until they are acknowledged over the public address system or by radio contact.[1] Not every fence on the course will have immediate first aid cover. It is vital that a Fence Judge knows what to do in the first few minutes following an accident while waiting for the emergency services to arrive. Seriously injured riders must be protected from further injury. If they are unconscious, or conscious but complaining of back or neck pain, they must not be moved unless it is vital to sustain life. The situations where this would be necessary are when breathing has stopped, or where the rider lies unconscious in water, or when an unconscious rider lying on their back starts vomiting. Whatever happens the rider's headgear should not be removed although it may be necessary to undo the chin strap. It may also be necessary to protect the rider from the sun, wind or rain.

With a fall of both horse and rider, the rider can be trapped underneath the horse. If there is any risk of further injury when the horse recovers and gets back up on to his feet, he must be prevented from doing so. This is achieved by sitting on the horse's head, but does need to be undertaken by someone who knows what they are doing and are confident about doing it. It is important that the person sits with their legs facing out from the top of the horse's head, i.e. the poll side. This will ensure, once the rider has been pulled clear and the horse may be released, the person getting up from the head and walking away does not sustain an injury by the horse as he struggles up. The last thing that is wanted at the scene of an accident is another injury!

When a horse is trapped on a fence, part of the obstacle may have to be dismantled in order to free the horse to prevent further injury. The Fence Repair Team must be summoned immediately by waving a white flag above head height. Most poles are secured by cord which can be cut with a sharp knife and Fence Judges themselves may do this while waiting for the Repair Team who will certainly be required to rebuild or re-rope the fence.

It is wise to study the fence carefully before the competition starts in order to understand what and where to cut in an

---

[1] Emergency flags: BHS, Rule 82.

Figure 25. Most fences can be dismantled easily.

emergency. Cutting all ropes in sight does not necessarily mean that the fence can be easily dismantled − or it may mean the entire lot falls down. Often a cut cord allows enough movement of a rail, albeit slight, to encourage the horse to jump free. Obstacles at which a horse is likely to be trapped have to be built in such a way that part of it can be quickly dismantled and be rebuilt exactly as before.[2]

[2] Nature of obstacles: FEI, Article 535 Para. 3.2. BHS, Rule 86(b).

CASE STUDY 8

Competition: *Intermediate One-Day Event*
Fence: *An upright wooden 'wall' of horizontal planks with a wide
   and deep ditch on the take-off side.*

*The combination came into the fence at near racing speed with the
horse being urged strongly forward with leg and whip. Standing off
the fence at an alarming distance and unable to gain any height, the
horse slammed straight into the wall. The rider was catapulted out of
the saddle to a heavy fall on the landing side while the horse fell on
to his back in the ditch. The near hind foot was wedged solidly
between two planks of the wall with much of the horse's weight
hanging on it.*

*Action taken: The course was immediately closed and the Vet
and Fence Repair Team called for to assist in releasing the horse.
(The rider had not sustained any injury other than a few bruises.)
The angle of the jammed hoof meant that it needed to be lifted
upwards first, before being pulled away. Advice to pull the foot
straight out was overruled by the Fence Judge as this would have
seriously damaged the foot. This was confirmed by the vet when
he arrived.*

*With leverage applied by the Fence Repair Team to obtain some
movement between the planks, the foot was lifted up and then out
with the aid of ropes. Once freed, the horse was able to struggle out
of the ditch and was then loaded in the horse ambulance to be taken
back to his box as he was lame.*

*The whole incident had been witnessed by the BHS Steward
who ordered the rider to report back to him to answer a charge of
dangerous riding. The Fence Judge also recorded the manner of riding
on the score sheet.*

The excessive pressing of an exhausted horse may lead to the
disqualification of a competitor.[3] In these circumstances Fence
Judges are not allowed to disqualify a rider themselves, but
must report the incident quickly to the Ground Jury (Three-Day
Event) via the Secretary. Any member of the Ground Jury who
witnesses such an incident has the authority to disqualify

[3] Abuse of horses: FEI, Article 521 Para. 1.

the competitor straight away. Cases of exhausted horses being pressed are rare — but it has happened at high levels of competition where the stakes are high and where the climatic conditions on the day are not particularly favourable to the horse. A Fence Judge does need to know the difference between a tired horse being quietly 'nursed' along and the distressed horse being pressed beyond his capabilities. The 'horseman's eye' distinguishes between the two. Many Fence Judges have a long involvement with horses at some level, although not necessarily eventing, and are able to make the judgement.

Sometimes a spectator will comment on the 'noise' made by the horse as he approaches, believing there is something wrong with his breathing. This is just 'high blowing', a flapping of the nostrils as the horse breathes out which is common among well-bred horses. Or a comment may be made about the flecks of foam falling from the horse's mouth on to his neck and shoulders. This, again, is quite normal. What, then, is an exhausted horse? He will look and sound such. The ears will no longer prick forward and the tail will no longer be 'carried'. Breathing will be harsh and laboured and the body will be streaked with lather. The rider will be working hard to keep the horse on a straight line, let alone trying to keep him in canter and not dropping back to a trot. Sadly, the time taken for a Fence Judge's observations to be reported, acknowledged and then acted on has sometimes been too late.

CASE STUDY 9

Competition: *World Equestrian Games — Official International Three-Day Event at four star level (CCIO****)*

Conditions: *Very hot with brilliant sunshine*
During the cross-country phase a horse was observed by Fence Judges to be distressed while negotiating an obstacle some half-way round the course. Some six fences further on the horse collapsed exhausted on the flat. He did not recover.

An apparently distressed horse may have 'second wind' and complete the course without harm. Also it is easy to be wise after the event. However, perhaps the 'system' may have failed to implement the procedures which allow a horse and rider combination to be stopped on the course (and timed) to enable a member of the Ground Jury to pronounce on the fitness or otherwise of the horse to proceed.

Following this fatality, there is now a greater awareness and concern at all levels of competition with regard to a tiring horse, particularly when climatic conditions are extreme. Once a Fence Judge has reported the condition of a horse, the horse's progress is monitored closely. Subsequent judges are specifically asked via radio contact to report on the manner in which the horse negotiates each obstacle. If there is any doubt about the fitness of the horse to continue, the next Fence Judge is instructed to stop the competitor.

A fence may be taken out of a competition for safety reasons. If this happens then all the faults which were incurred at the obstacle, except elimination, are taken away.[4]

Up until 1992, when a rider had to dismount in order for a trapped horse to be freed, the time that he was held up was not recorded at One or Two-Day Events. At a Three-Day Event, however, the Fence Judge must time the rider from the moment he is instructed to dismount until he restarts after being told that he may do so. With the introduction of the amendment to the BHS Rules in 1993, this now applies to all events. This hold-up time is deducted from the overall time that the competitor takes to complete the course, to give an adjusted time.[5]

With a horse or rider lying injured on the take-off or landing side of a fence, the obstacle is impassable. As in the case of a horse trapped on a fence, the competition must be stopped immediately and this must be done safely and fairly. If the course is blocked, for whatever reason, a fourth, orange flag is used simultaneously with the call for services. Oncoming competitors must be flagged down and stood aside. Their hold-up time is recorded on the Fence Judge's official watch from the moment they pass a timing marker to the moment they are restarted and pass the marker again.[6] The stopping drill is

[4] Modification of course: BHS, Rule 84.
[5] Competitors in difficulty: FEI, Article 533 Para. 6.3. BHS, Rule 78.
[6] Stopping competitors: FEI, Article 533 Para. 7. BHS, Rule 7.

often of great concern, not only to Fence Judges, but also to competitors. It is most important that the procedure is carried out correctly and that the time is recorded. If the time is not taken then the competitor cannot have his overall time for the course adjusted and any chance of winning a place in the competition has been lost.

A Fence Judge stops an oncoming competitor because the fence is impassable, dangerous, or significantly altered in outline (a top rail broken or dislodged, for example), or because Control request it. If it is at all possible, Control will try to stop competitors before they reach the fence where the accident has occurred. For this last reason, any Fence Judge may be asked to stop one or more competitors at his fence, although Control will try to use obstacles which have been designated beforehand as Stopping Fences. This means that they are straightforward, single fences, a brush for example, which a competitor will find easier to jump after a hold-up which will have broken their rhythm. However, it is not always possible to use these particular fences and a rider may be stopped at any obstacle.

Each Fence Judge is provided with an official BHS digital watch to record the stop and re-start times of competitors held up on the cross-country course. The digits which appear in the display record minutes, seconds and one-hundreths of a second. The last two figures are ignored and are usually 'masked' by a patch of adhesive paper. (Hundredths of a second are not required).

There are two buttons, one on the top left and one on the top right of the watch (Figure 26). The only one which 'works' is that on the left, as the watch has been 'doctored' so that the right-hand button does not function. The watch does not display the actual time of day, only the passage of time. When it is running the digits are seen to turn over as each second passes. This is the state, or mode, it should be in when not in use, i.e. when the watch is strung around the Fence Judge's neck.

Although the figures on the face can be immobilised by pressing the left-hand button in order to mark a particular moment in time, the watch itself continues to tick over inside. When the button is pressed again to unfreeze the figures they immediately leap forward to catch up with the time elapsed.

The important thing is to keep calm. First check that the figures on the watch are changing over. If they are not, press

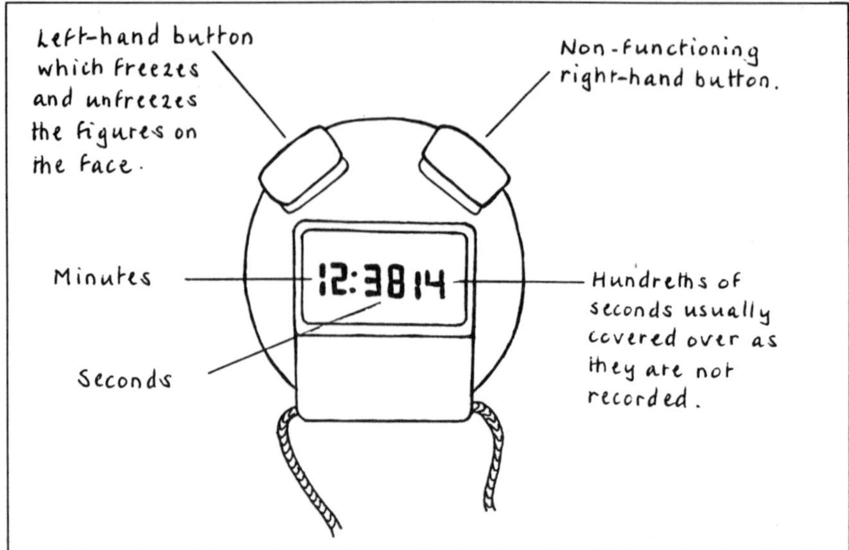

Figure 26. Fence Judge's timing watch.

the top left-hand button so that they are. As the competitor passes the timing marker placed some 100 paces in front of the fence, the top left-hand button is pressed to freeze the figures on the watch face. Once this is done, and not before, the Fence Judge walks out in front of the fence waving the red flag towards the competitor at waist height together with loud calls of 'Stop'.

Competitors are clearly briefed on this signal and failure to stop means they are liable to be eliminated at the discretion of the BHS Steward (One and Two-Day Events) or the Ground Jury (Three-Day Events). If the flag is waved above head height (the signal that the doctor is required) then the competitor could possible ignore it. But riders are usually very sensible.

It does help to be prepared for these situations by having the red flag to hand at all times. If it is not, then, invariably, when it is required it will be on the far side of the fence or the furthest distance away it could possibly be. A good idea is to tuck it in a belt on your person so it is always immediately available.

Once the competitor has been stopped, he is quietly re-assured that his stop time has been recorded. The timing marker is pointed out to him and he is told that he will be given fair warning when the course is clear and he may re-start. While competitors are being held on the clock, they may dismount and relax.

Figure 27. Competitors may dismount.

Only the four left-hand figures are written in the 'Remarks' column of the score sheet against the competitor's number, e.g. Horse 126 Stopped at 0831. These figures should be confirmed by the co-judge before the button is pressed to re-set the watch, when the figures will leap forward to the time elapsed and start running again. If, at this moment, a second competitor appears on the horizon making a bee-line for your fence – do not panic! Go through exactly the same stopping procedure as before. The watch is not an ordinary stopwatch (which is restricted to recording one horse at a time) and any number of competitors can be 'held' on it. With two, or more, horses held at a fence care must be taken to ensure that the correct times are recorded against the appropriate competitors.

Competitors may only be re-started when Control gives the instruction to do so. A certain co-judge admits to acting prematurely on this during his early fence judging days. With two competitors held at the fence, the instruction to re-start came from Control. As the first horse cleared the fence, the second rider called out, 'Shall I go too?' 'I would if I were you', replied the co-judge. The judge with the watch turned a paler shade of grey. Too late now to stop them as they galloped for the fence, so it was a question of re-setting the watch quickly to record the second start time. Later on in the competition it was learnt that, some two fences further on, both the competitors went up the steps neatly as a pair! Of course, the second horse should not have been re-started until advised by Control when the first one was well clear.

Once the course is clear and the go-ahead to re-start has been received, then the rider is instructed to go back past the timing marker. They may canter a couple of circles to warm up and must be given a flying start. As they gallop past the marker the figures on the watch are frozen again and the combination is judged through the fence before the second time is recorded on the score sheet, e.g. Horse 126 Re-started at 1020. Again, this should be checked before the watch is reset ready for the next emergency. It is essential that the watch is checked regularly throughout the day to ensure that the figures are changing over. It is very easy for the button to be pressed inadvertantly so that the figures are already frozen!

Now and again, an instruction to stop a horse may come after the timing marker has been passed. On one such occasion there had been a crashing fall at a fence towards the end of the course. The following competitor, not so far behind, was approaching the fence immediately before the one with the emergency when the order to stop them came over the radio. The time had to be taken from one of the posts holding the ropes marking the course some 20 metres in front of the fence. Although it had been a late stop, the competitor was pleased that they did not have far to go back down the course to re-start.

In preparation for stopping situations it is wise to listen to commentary over the public address system or the radio, and to watch the next fence after yours if it is in view. If you know the next fence has had an accident you are alerted to the possibility that you may be asked to stop the next competitor. Sometimes, of course, Fence Judges may take it upon themselves to stop a competitor because the next fence has an emergency. This is usually the case later on in the course where a faster rider is steadily gaining on a slower one.

CASE STUDY 10

Competition: *Intermediate One-Day Event*
Fence 15: *A straightforward brush at the top of a steep slope leading down to the next fence.*
Fence 16: *An imposing palisade with a ditch on the take-off side and a considerable drop on the landing side.*
The first competitor hit the palisade hard which resulted in a heavy fall for both horse and rider on the landing side of the fence. With both horse and rider down and the Fence Judge racing for flags, a second competitor galloped into view. As all flags were now waved to summon services to the scene of the accident, the Fence Judge at the brush stopped and held the second rider. This took further pressure off the judges below who could immediately turn all their attention to the fallen horse and rider. It made life easier for the second competitor too. Far better to be held at an easier fence to jump first once they were re-started.

Practice with the watch makes perfect! Any competitor, for instance, can be timed past the marker and, once they have jumped the fence and been scored, the figures can be checked and the watch re-set.

At a Three-Day Event competitors may be stopped at a designated Stopping Point on the course. Just as with the Timing Point in front of a fence, the time of a competitor is taken as they gallop past the Stopping Point, not after the competitor has stopped and not after a standing start.[7]

---

[7] Stopping competitors: FEI, Article 533 Para. 7.5.

7 · 'FENCE 9 TO CONTROL': COMMUNICATIONS

The principal means of communication, viz. the use of flags, whistle and radio, are explained by the BHS Official at every Fence Judge's Briefing. A highlight for any Fence Judge is to be asked to report on the obstacle, and sometimes others as well, using a radio. Briefing will cover which button to press in order to transmit. More important is to know when not to press the button and so ensure good communications. The cardinal rule is not to transmit when somebody else is on the air. Listen first, then send your message. If every one sends messages simultaneously, nobody will hear a thing, other than a garbled, electrical noise. No one should transmit when another person is speaking.

The most important task for a radio operator is to help in the event of an emergency. A second task is the reporting upon the progress of competitors to the Controller and Commentator. Messages should be brief and to the point, e.g. 'Horse 72 clear Fence 10 direct route' or 'Horse 76 first refusal Fence 12 at second element'. Waxing lyrical may give the ego a boost, especially if the Commentator repeats your words over the public address system, but someone may have an emergency at their fence. When an accident is reported, keep off the air until Control say that normal reporting may continue. Emergency talk takes priority over commentary talk. Other judges with radios may need to be informed by Control to stop oncoming horses.

In the event of a calamity at an obstacle, the radio is often the only life-line to Control and it is important to keep Control fully informed, e.g. 'Fence 10, horse 78 has fallen, horse and rider are down. Over.' The word 'over' means that a reply is awaited.

Figure 28. Do not transmit at the same time as everyone else.

Control will want to know the state of horse and rider. Follow up the message as soon as possible, e.g. 'Fence 10, horse up, rider still on ground. Doctor required, the course is blocked. Over.' It is at this point that Control will probably instruct other radio operators to stop competitors who are approaching their fences, and to 'hold' the start. If there is an emergency at another fence and you have been told to stop the next horse at your fence then acknowledge the message and inform Control as soon as the horse has been stopped, e.g. 'Message received to stop next horse at Fence 7', followed by 'Horse 80 stopped at Fence 7. Out.' The word 'out' is used to indicate that you do not expect a reply. Control will instruct you when to re-start the horse. Acknowledge and inform Control once the horse has been re-started and is clear of your fence, e.g. 'Horse 80 re-started and now clear at Fence 7. Out.' For normal brief messages the words 'Over' and 'Out' are not necessary. When reporting on other fences besides your own it is important that everyone involved is in clear sight of the others. The radio must be kept with the reporter at all times. Never leave it unattended or put it down, even if you have to assist in an emergency, otherwise a vital message may be missed. Also, the weight of the radio is enough to press the transmit button, and heaven only knows what may be broadcast! The net is an open one and all operators

THE BRITISH HORSE SOCIETY — FAULTS AT CROSS-COUNTRY OBSTACLES   Class N

Obstacle No. 14   Judge LOWE   Sheet No. 12

HORSE NO.	CLEAR	1st refusal run-out or circle	2nd refusal etc.	3rd refusal etc.	Falls of horse and/or rider	Omission of obstacle or boundary flag, error of course not rectified, unauthorised assistance	TOTAL PENALTY POINTS	REMARKS (if any)
	✓	20	40	Elimination	60	Elimination		
32	✓						✓	
102		20			60		80	Horse refused at B, rider fell
34		20					20	Crossed tracks between A and B
103		20	40	E			E	
35	✓						✓	Stopped at 21.04 Restarted 23.16
?	✓						✓	Grey horse. Blue rider.

Figure 29. An example of a score sheet. (Sheet reproduced by kind permission of the BHS Horse Trials Group.)

can hear what other operators are saying. In addition, the entire radio net will be blocked the moment a *bona fide* message is transmitted. Radios do not work very well, if at all, once they are wet. In wet weather the radio should be covered with a plastic bag — this is very effective.

A Fence Judge communicates the scores of each competitor to the Scorers on official score sheets which are collected by 'runners'. There are pairs of sheets, usually a white top sheet with a green sheet behind it. The top sheet is torn off and handed over to the runners when they come to collect them and not before. The copy is kept by the Fence Judge. Sheets must always be handed to the runner when called for even if they are not full. This assists the Scorers who have the mammoth task of checking and adding up the scores of each competitor before writing them up on the score boards. If a Fence Judge hangs on to a sheet then the final scores of riders will be delayed. With the scores of several hundred competitors over some twenty-odd fences to be added up throughout the day, Scorers like to be supplied regularly with score sheets. Competitors, too, like to see their scores as soon as possible.

The score sheets are self-carbonating. It is important to remember to insert the pressure card behind each pair of sheets before marking the top one. Failure to do this means that the whole book is used up for the first seven horses. Marking is done with a pencil or a ball-point pen, although the latter tends to give up in damp or wet conditions. It is best for Fence Judges to be out on their feet to judge a competitor through a fence and not to be sitting inside a vehicle. This is not always practical. Score sheets seem to be designed to disintegrate even in the lightest shower of rain. The judge marking down the scores may need to remain sheltered inside the vehicle during wet weather so that score sheets remain intact and legible. Judges are asked to write in capital letters for obvious reasons — some handwriting resembles that found on some doctors̗ prescriptions!

The fence number, the judge's name, the class (N for Novice, I for Intermediate and A for Advanced) and the number of the sheet are written at the top of each sheet in the space provided. The number of each competitor is recorded as he jumps, or attempts to jump, the obstacle and any penalties incurred are written in the appropriate columns. If a competitor jumps clear then both the 'clear' and 'total' columns are ticked (Figure 29).

Scorers prefer ticks and not zeros. A zero only needs a mark to appear next to it to look like the figure 10. Time and effort is wasted in having this checked out with the Fence Judge.

A competitor's number must never be written down until it has been seen. Competitors do not necessarily come in programme order and a rider heading towards your fence may have overtaken another competitor. Sometimes it can be difficult to see a competitor's number, particularly if the sun is shining brightly on the rider's tabard. Numbers can be seen more easily on the outside rather than the inside of a bend, and one judge needs to take up a position where it is easiest to observe numbers. If a number is missed it is vital that it is not guessed at. A question-mark is put in the 'Number' column and if possible, some sort of description in the 'Remarks' column, e.g. chestnut horse — rider green with white spots. Scorers are able to pick up the competitor's number quite easily from the score sheets of the previous fence and the one after. If a guess is made by a Fence Judge and it is wrong, then it makes life difficult for Scorers, and, of course, it has to be checked out with the Fence Judge.

Diagrams are important where cross tracks, in particular, are awarded. Any doubts about a judgement should be noted with a description of the circumstances. Scorers will pass the information to the Steward who will then come down to the fence and discuss the incident. If there is not enough room to document everything in the 'Remarks' column then either use several more sections on the score sheet, or refer to continued notes on the back of the sheet, remembering to add the competitor's number to any diagram etc. However, anything written on the reverse of the top sheet needs to be copied on to the reverse of the second sheet so that there is a duplicate record. This is most important. Top copies have been known to disappear without any trace, perhaps blown out of the runner's bag or whatever. The only record of any penalties awarded or not at any obstacle then lies with the Fence Judge who has the bottom copy.

Score sheets should not be torn off until the score collector calls for them. Lodging a sheet underneath a windscreen wiper or some object is not recommended — at the very least they can be forgotten and 'overlooked' and at the very worst they blow away across the parkland in the westerly gale which is bound to be blowing at the time! There is one Fence Judge who will admit to putting a top copy in a pocket. The sheet was eventually deemed as 'lost' and the duplicate called for. After returning home, the lost sheet was found, much to the embarrassment of the judge concerned.

Fence Judges must not leave the fence after the last horse has been through until the final score sheet has been collected. This may be a little while after the last competitor, depending on the position of the fence. Use the time to check that the area around an obstacle is free of litter and no piece of equipment has been overlooked. It is very easy to forget the rake which you have kept in a safe place, and then find you have to come all the way back for it!

It has been known for a Fence Judge to leave the obstacle with both copies of the last score sheet and return home without waiting for clearance to be given. Fence Judges are requested to wait at least half an hour after the final scores are put up in case of any queries or objections to a judgement. In one particular case, at a Three-Day Event, all the judges were kept long after this because one Fence Judge went straight home complete with the last score sheet! After a long day at an obstacle it was not particularly amusing to those who complied with the rules.

8 · TAKE-OFFS AND LANDINGS

A main responsibility of a Fence Judge is the safety of competitors at a cross-country obstacle. With this in mind, it is expected that the ground around a fence is cared for as described in the BHS pamphlet *Instructions to Fence Judges*, i.e. holes must be filled in by treading in if the ground gets cut up. Badly poached ground around an obstacle will cause some strain to a horse when he jumps and on the landing side of a fence it may contribute to a fall. Ground that is badly cut up on the take-off side may encourage refusals, especially with small-footed or novice horses. Considering fairness, as well as safety, both take-offs and landings must be looked after. Competitors can rightly expect, within reason, that the going into and away from an obstacle should be much the same throughout a competition.

The amount of effort required to ensure this depends on the type of fence and the terrain, as much as on the weather. The weather is often a crucial factor, particularly when there is an 'unexpected' deluge. Perfect conditions are rare. The permanent grassland with its springy turf found in parklands of this country is better able to withstand wear and tear and it usually drains well. Clay in wet conditions, on the other hand, can be an 'out on your feet all day' situation and repair may be needed after almost every competitor to avoid deterioration, which can build up all too quickly. Soft patches can develop into a bog after many horses have been through. This can particularly be the case with a narrow fence which has no alternatives. Although the ground may be fine in the morning, after many horses have used the same spot for take-off under worsening conditions, it will have become a quagmire by mid-afternoon. A competitor having problems at an obstacle can cut up the ground as if a

Figure 30. Look after the take-off.

cavalry charge had been through.

Any divots which have been scooped out by the horse should be replaced and trodden in. Drop fences in particular can mean that material is dug out and flung backwards by the hind hooves as the horse lowers himself down. Treading in alone may not be enough and a spade can be useful in dealing with deep hoof holes. Newly laid turf will not have settled and on slopes it can be continually dug up. The Fence Judge will be kept busy replacing pieces of turf. Light soils require only occasional raking. Attention is needed to ensure that take-offs are not being lowered, which effectively raises the height of the obstacle, or that ground lines are not being altered as earth heaps up against them. A foot, or better still a yard broom, quickly removes soil which piles up on the lower rail of a fence. Sometimes the ground on the landing side of a fence can be pressed down after many horses have landed on it. As a result the level may be lowered and this can be dangerous on drop fences. Call Fence Repair to put more material down. Whatever 'repairs' may be necessary, it is vital to watch out for an oncoming competitor. A Fence Judge has to take opportunities as they arise, but be careful!

CASE STUDY 11

Competition: *Novice One-Day Event*
Fence: *Water complex with an uphill approach consisting of two substantial steps down to the water and a step out.*

There had been a fall on the landing side of the previous fence and the horse had made a bee-line back to the horse box park. The rider, uninjured, set off on foot to retrieve the horse. The Fence Judges at the water seized this opportunity of a short 'break' to carry out repairs to the second step which was constantly being churned up. Down below the first step, the approach to the fence was out of view.

Meanwhile, back at the horse boxes, someone had caught the horse and trotted it quickly back in hand to its unseated rider. The rider remounted and set off smartly towards the water. Only the whistle of the previous Fence Judge warned the judges working on the step and they managed to scramble out of the way in time, albeit in a somewhat undignified manner!

Moral to be learnt here? Never assume that a horse and rider will not be reunited very quickly, and always have someone watch your back!

It is also important to take care where tools, such as a rake, are kept. They will need to be close to hand but must not be anywhere where they may interfere with the horse's progress. There is particularly a danger of this if a horse has run out and swings back round to approach the fence again. Tools are best kept leaning up against the vehicle and not flat on the ground.

Care does not end with raking or treading in holes. As a competition progresses, stones or flints may be unearthed to turn a hoof. They may also cut or bruise a horse's foot and must be cleared away. Strange objects have been known to rise to the surface under continual pounding of many hooves. At an event being held on the site of an old army camp, the Fence Judge noticed ammunition which was being kicked up on the landing side of the fence. Raking produced hundreds of rounds of ammunition which turned out to be spent and not live! Apparently a box had been buried there and this had broken apart with the number of horses galloping over it.

In the same way, roots may be exposed to trip the unsuspecting, and these must also be dealt with either by the Fence Judge or the Fence Repair Team (who will need to be called for).

Clay in wet conditions becomes very sticky and holding, and a shoe can easily be wrenched off. The same problem also exists in places where there is no grass covering, such as woodland areas. The ground can become deep and holding because it does not normally drain very well, and it is easy for a shoe to be lost. A sharp eye will notice the wrenched-off shoe and it is very important to retrieve any that are lost. This is not only in the interests of safety, because the shoe will inevitably have nails protruding from it like a pincushion, but also because many competitors are grateful to have them returned, particularly if it is a therapeutic shoe individually tailored to the horse. Of course, many shoes are so twisted and distorted that they are of no use to anyone. It is amazing the number of 'sculptures' which can be amassed by the end of the season.

Slippery going can be dangerous. This can especially be a problem when there is a sudden downpour during a competition after a long dry spell. The ground will be hard and the water will just lie on the top, making the ideal conditions for slipping and skidding. There may not be much a Fence Judge can do. Sometimes Fence Repair may be able to put some material down like stonedust, particularly in soft ground, to reduce slipperiness.

Water jumps pose unique problems. Even with the best base in the country, soft patches and holes may develop after several competitors have been through. After a fall in water, some riders are convinced that an enormous hole exists — careful investigation proves it either way. A Fence Judge needs to check the bottom fairly regularly and especially so after a fall or if the horse appears to peck or stumble. Remember that shoes can also be lost in water!

Calm water also reflects images. No horse wishes to jump on a human, even if it is only the brightly coloured reflection of a Fence Judge! Falls in water, on rare occasions, may be attributed to mirror-like reflections.

Figure 31. Check for holes.

CASE STUDY 12

Competition: *Novice One-Day Event*

Fence: *Water complex consisting of a drop into a pond followed by a steep slope out. The pond lay in a steeply sided 'bowl' covered with trees and rhododendron bushes. The approach was down a narrow 'gully' which ended in the drop.*

In the brilliant sunlight the calm surface of the pond reflected the surrounding vegetation clearly as well as the figure of a person standing on the opposite slope which gave a clear view of the fence. Their colourful reflection appeared on the exact spot where the average horse would land. Five out of the first six horses fell in the water.

Action taken: *After discussion, the Technical Adviser called for sand to be put down in front of the drop. As a horse approached the jump a fine shower of sand was kicked forward so destroying the images in the water. This technique meant that there would be no danger of reflections for the rest of the competition. There were no further falls at the obstacle.*

The effect of the sun on a particular fence can be important at different times of the day. This applies especially when a horse jumps from bright sunshine into the darkness of a wood. Shadows can cause optical illusions. Fence Judges need to be aware of the sun's changing position.

The water splashed as a horse jumps out of water can soften the ground on the landing side. Experience has proved that this is best left alone as attempts to tread in usually only make matters worse. The construction of the landing tends to keep the ground fairly compact and it· is only large holes which need to be dealt with. The Fence Repair Team can always be called for to put down small grade stones, sand, etc.

After an accident which has not rendered the fence impassable, it is also important to ensure that vehicles, including ambulances, do not park in front of or behind the fence. The course must be kept clear for oncoming competitors.

Sometimes a fence may be taken out of a competition for reasons of safety. When this happens, all faults incurred by competitors at that obstracle are taken away, except elimination.

Both horse and rider approach a fence on trust, and this trust must not be abused.

Figure 32. Keep the landing side clear.

9 · 'CLEAR THE COURSE, PLEASE!'

The cross-country course must be kept safe for both competitors and spectators. Judges are responsible for ensuring that all the approach routes to, and the exit routes from, an obstacle are kept clear for oncoming competitors.

Competitors will have walked the course in order to work out the fastest routes between obstacles and the best line of approach to each of them. Fence Judges need to be aware of the location of the fences immediately before and after the one being judged. Careful observation and discussion will ensure that all the options and alternative tracks through the fence which are available to the rider are thoroughly understood. Many spectators or visitors to the obstacle may be quite unaware of what these are. Walking the fence through the 'eyes' of a rider, indeed those of a horse, always helps to earmark the usual line which a competitor may elect to take.

Where there are ropes lining the course, the task of keeping spectators off the rider's track is made easier. Once a competition is under way no one, with the exception of a competitor walking the course, should be inside the ropes. This includes the hordes of followers who may accompany the rider! At a Three-Day Event it is forbidden under penalty of disqualification to inspect the obstacles or the course before they are officially shown to the competitors. After the course has been officially shown, competitors are free to revisit the course and examine the fences. Although the course may be roped, it does not always mean that the Fence Judge's task is an easy one.

CASE STUDY 13

Competition: *Three-Day Event*
Fence: *A coffin consisting of three elements*
The roping around the fence itself as well as along the track of the course leading up to and away from it was extensive and effective. However, a narrow gap had been left between thick shrubs beyond the penalty zone of the landing side of the last element. There were no compulsory markers which competitors were obliged to pass. (Where red and white flags mark a compulsory passage on the course riders must pass between them, with the red flag on the right and the white flag on their left.[1] Omission of a compulsory passage, or passing through in the wrong order, means elimination at the discretion of the Ground Jury or BHS Steward.)[2] Any rider going out through the gap could effectively cut off a loop in the track and save considerable time (Figure 33). This was not, of course, the intention of the course designer!

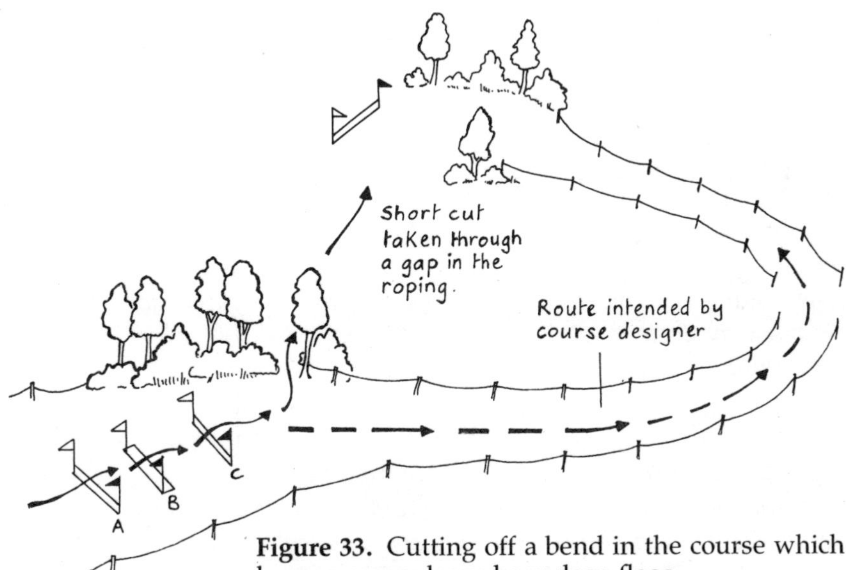

Figure 33. Cutting off a bend in the course which has no compulsory boundary flags.

The Fence Judges at the coffin were warned by the Ground Jury that one competitor had made it clear that they intended to take the 'short cut'. This was quite legal in the circumstances and certainly it

[1] Marking of the course: FEI, Article 534 Para 1.1. BHS, Rule 83.
[2] Additional reasons for eliminations: FEI, Article 533 Para. 3. BHS, Rule 83.

was impossible to put up extra roping or to introduce compulsory boundary flags now that competitors had walked the course and the competition was well under way. It did mean, however, that the Fence Judges were able to make sure that no spectators stood in the gap — a favourite spot for many to stand in until that moment as it gave a clear view of the obstacle. Eventually this imaginative rider came along, jumped the fence and duly nipped out through the gap!

Where little or no roping exists, extra vigilance is required. An alternative approach to the obstacle may look like an idyllic picnic spot, but it is wise to explain clearly the potential drama which may occur if the group remains there and to ask them to move — even if no competitor has taken that route all morning! It is always gratifying when the next rider proves the point and endows the Fence Judge with psychic powers. The general public enjoy being informed and they, along with the majority of competitors walking the course, respond happily to clear instructions.

CASE STUDY 14

Competition: One-Day Advanced
Fence: *A water complex*
The roping around the fence was limited. The approach from the previous obstacle was along a substantial, mature hedge with trees and with a barbed wire fence in front. In order to come in on a straight approach to the first element of the water complex taking the direct line through, competitors made a sharp turn round the right-angled corner of the hedge (Figure 34).

With the fence so open to spectators, it was vital that a sharp eye was kept on those people who walked along the hedgerow directly facing the water. Any horse approaching from the previous obstacle was completely unsighted by anyone standing in this position. The fact that the water complex was later on in the course also meant that competitors were often gaining on each other so two horses could be relatively close together.

It was in this very situation that a small group of spectators stood against the hedgerow looking down directly to the first element of the water. The first horse jumped through clear. The group immediately started to walk away from the hedge towards the water. Loud whistles halted them in their tracks and then, in obedience to the signals and instructions given, all except one went back against the line of the hedge.. The second horse hurtled round the corner and jumped clear through the direct route of the complex.

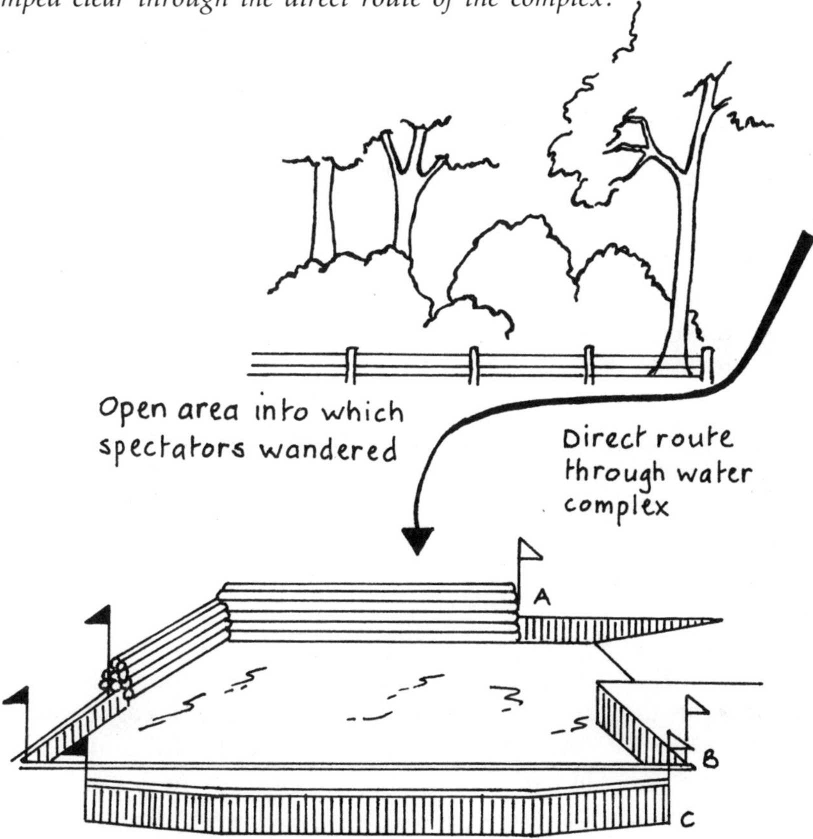

Figure 34. Watch out for spectators.

The one spectator who did not go back flat against the hedge? Well, he came down somewhat shaken to apologise, say thank you, and to comment, 'I now know what you meant. I really felt the wind of the horse passing.' It had been very close.

At this same competition the following year, extensive roping of the fence and its approach eliminated the problem and the Fence Judges concerned experienced no more nightmares of spectators strung up in a line on barbed wire fences!

Warnings to clear the course can only be by voice or whistle — often both are necessary. Whistles should be blown regularly and robustly, ideally when the combination lands over the previous fence. The next obstacle, which may be out of view, becomes accustomed to the rhythm of your signal. If only for this reason, whistles must be blown — even if there is no other soul in sight! Sometimes the siting of a fence means that the Fence Judge there has no other advanced warning of an approaching competitor other than the whistle of the previous obstacle. Care must be taken, however, not to rely solely on the previous Fence Judge's signal or you may be lulled into a sense of false security! It may not be blown for some reason — perhaps the judge forgets, or the pea has stuck, or lunch has just been delivered! Always keep a sharp lookout as well. Remember that some spectators may be hard of hearing and a few may even be deaf. Voice and whistle may not be heard. In these situations, their attention must be sought by some other means — either by going across to them personally or by signalling clearly. Above all, it is another aspect which Fence Judges need to be aware of.

Very young children and the elderly cannot be expected to move with the speed of Olympic sprinters. Warnings should allow them time to clear the course without panic. Always advise spectators when it is best not to cross the course by being aware where the next horse is on the course. Far better to ask them to wait for the next competitor to clear the fence and then allow them to cross over safely and calmly instead of possibly having to make an undignified dash for it. In addition, it can break the concentration of competitors if they see people suddenly fleeing in all directions out of their path, let alone if they themselves have to yell at them to do so!

Spectators must be treated with firmness in the interests of safety, but it should be done with politeness and diplomacy. They have every right to attend an event and as the paying public they are essential to the future of the sport. Fence Judges are as much ambassadors for the sport as anyone else involved in the competition. Sometimes, of course, it may be necessary to shout at someone in the heat of the moment as horse and rider bear down towards the fence, but do explain afterwards why it was necessary. Remember, also, that many spectators do not have very much experience of horses and will not understand fully the implications of their actions. However, they are interested enough to attend the event, so always be ready to inform them and to discuss any queries they may have in order that they may understand and enjoy the sport fully.

Cameras must not be positioned in such a way that they could possibly interfere with the progress of a competitor. The 'professionals' will always discuss the siting of themselves and their equipment with the Fence Judge. Again, it is most important to understand the alternative routes which are available to the competitor. 'Amateurs' with cameras can be more of a problem. Many will try to get too close to the fence and should be asked to stand back. No flash should be used because it could take away the rider's and/or the horse's concentration, and could lead to a refusal or to a fall. A Fence Judge needs to be alert to this danger where the course swings sharply away on the landing side of the obstacle to be jumped. Spectators standing on the outside of the bend can appear as a wall of people to the horse as he approaches the fence. They must keep quiet and still. Check with the owner that any camera in evidence will not flash when used.

No one other than an official is allowed to stand inside the penalty zone of a Three-Day Event.

'Runners' regularly visit each fence throughout the day to collect the top copy of the Fence Judge's score sheet to take back to the official Scorers. Collections may be by motorbike or by riders, and the latter are usually members of the Pony Club. They do a marvellous job but a careful watch must be kept to ensure that they do not cross the course at the wrong moment or place themselves too close to the fence. After a few visits a rhythm is established and runners soon recognise the Fence Judge's signals and become aware of all the routes the competitors are taking.

Dogs can be everyone's nightmare. The ruling is explicit — all dogs must be kept on leads during the competition.[3] Attention is drawn to this rule in the printed programme and also over the public address system throughout the day. Despite this, loose dogs are regularly found on cross-country courses while the competition is in progress. Some are with their 'minder', some have managed to slip their lead while tied up in the horse box park or the car park. They present a very real danger to both

---

[3] Safety precautions: BHS, Rule 7.

Figure 35. All dogs must be on leads.

horse and rider. A horse travelling at speed and 'colliding' with a dog which runs out to 'worry' it can be brought down in the most horrific fall for both horse and rider. It will almost certainly do the dog no good either. Everybody loves their dog, so take extra care of it on the cross-country course!

Fence Judge's must use their authority to insist that any loose dog is put on a lead immediately.

Dogs on yards of lead can also impose problems. Although they are basically 'anchored' in one sense, they still have enough freedom to make life difficult. A Fence Judge with his ankles tied by several 'wraps around' by such a dog is only one problem! It is wise to ask the owner to wind the dog in. Some competitors walking the course do not seem fully to appreciate the rule concerning dogs. This applies to the first-time novice right up to the advanced International competitor who should, by now, know better! At the water, for example, it has been known on a hot summer's afternoon for dogs to be let off their leads to have a swim and cool off while the competition is in progress. In one such instance, a competitor walking the course led her dog down to the water's edge and asked sweetly, 'You don't mind if he cools off for a moment do you?' Before the Fence Judge could answer equally sweetly, the lead was removed and the dog was loose in the water and swimming in the middle of the water jump. 'Oh, you do mind', the competitor said before she was asked nicely to retrieve the dog. It may all sound pretty harmless. However, one of the Fence Judges had to race into position in order to stop the next competitor on the course if the dog had not been retrieved and the fence was not clear. In this case the dog was recaptured and the rider did not have to be stopped. If they had been it would certainly not have been very fair. A rule is a rule and this one is of paramount importance. It has been said that the owners of a dog which may have contributed to a serious injury of horse and/or rider may be liable in law. The odd Fence Judge who allows his dog to go for a swim in the water in between competitors jumping through it is not setting a good example by disobeying the rules! A dog may well be Supreme Obedience Champion from the year dot — it still must be on a lead while horses are running. A length of twine in your pocket has its uses for dogs with no lead. When an owner is challenged and says he has no lead, give him the twine; end of scenario. However, do not expect your twine to be returned — it never is! Of course, a length of twine enables you to 'capture' a loose dog which has lost its owner. With the dog tied to the bull-bar of the Land Rover it is at least safe and you can only hope that the owner listens to the public address system and turns up soon! (Otherwise you know you will be soft enough to give it some of your lunch.)

10 · THE INS AND OUTS OF PENALTY ZONES

The penalty zone is an area marked out round each cross-country obstacle at a Three-Day Event. They are not used at other events. The zone extends 10 metres in front and 20 metres beyond the fence and to a width of 10 metres from the ends of each obstacle which are marked by the red and white boundary flags. If a fence has an alternative part to it, the zone extends at least 20 metres beyond all the parts that a competitor may attempt to jump (Figure 36).[1]

A combination fence or adjacent fences that are sited closely together and which would have overlapping zones are surrounded by only one penalty zone. This area extends continuously from 10 metres in front of the first element or obstacle to 20 metres beyond the last element or obstacle. The boundary of the area on either side of every element or obstacle within the zone follows the course of the track and extends to 10 metres each side of it.

Penalty zones are marked with pegs for the guidance of competitors and the Fence Judge. The lines between pegs may be marked with chalk, paint or scorched grass to make the limits of the area clearer, or by any other means as long as it does not obstruct the competitor. No one is allowed inside the zone except the Fence Judge or other Officials, and they must make quite sure they are not in a position which could impede the competitor in any way.[2] In addition, no television camera or photographer must be in a position where they might obstruct horse and rider. The photographers will be clearly labelled with accreditation cards which permit them, as professionals, to take

[1] Penalty zone: FEI, Article 536 Para. 4.
[2] Penalty zone: FEI, Article 536 Para. 8.

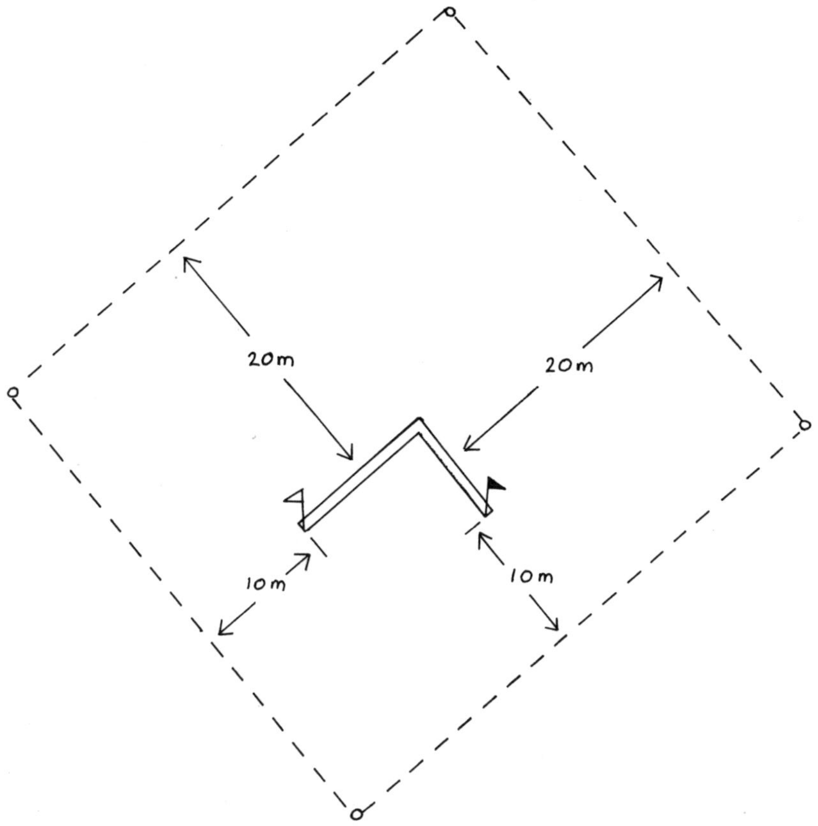

Figure 36. The dimensions of a penalty zone.

photographs on the course. Anyone else has to remain behind the course ropes. It has been known for cameras to be strapped to the fence in order to obtain a dramatic shot or an unusual angle. As long as this does not interfere with the competitor in any way and clearance is sought for and given by the Technical Delegate or Steward, it can be allowed.

No judgement takes place until the competitor has entered the penalty zone. Once a competitor has entered he may be penalised for refusals, crossed tracks, circles and falls. However, if a fall occurs outside the zone, even if it is as a direct result of the manner in which the fence was jumped, it is not penalised and it also does not count in the number of falls which add up to elimination.[3] Competitors will try to 'hang on' until they are outside the penalty zone.

[3] Penalty zone: FEI, Article 536 Para. 5.

Figure 37. Judgement begins when the competitor enters the zone.

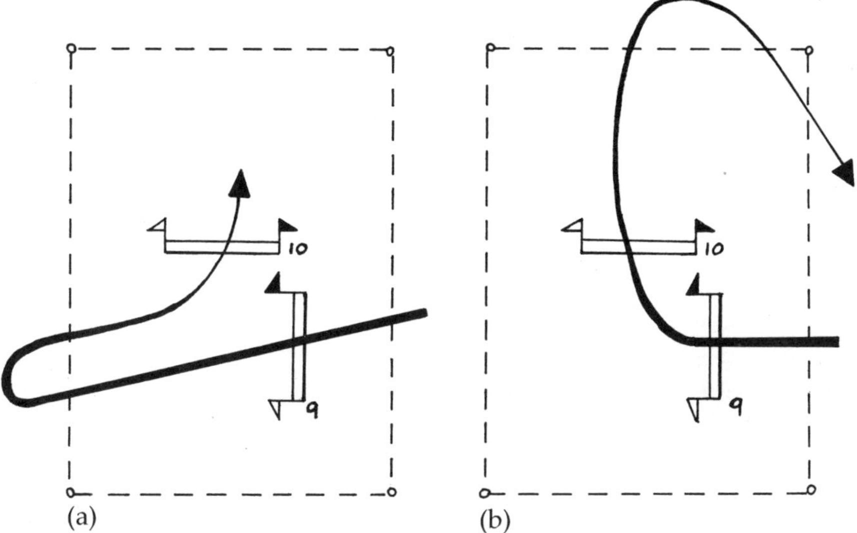

Figure 38. Leaving the penalty zone: (a) 10 penalties; (b) 0 panalties.

Once a competitor has entered the penalty zone, he must stay inside until the last obstacle or element in the zone has been jumped. Leaving the zone before this has been achieved is penalised by 10 penalties, although it does not count as any form of disobedience. A competitor is judged to have left the zone if the horse has crossed beyond the limits of the zone with all four feet (Figure 38a).[4] Once a competitor has jumped the last obstacle or element, however, he is allowed to leave and re-enter the zone without incurring faults (Figure 38b).[5]

In addition, if a competitor has incurred penalties at the fence (for a refusal, run-out, circle or fall) he may leave the penalty zone, without incurring any additional faults, in order to negotiate the obstacle. In some situations, particularly those which involve more than one fence or option, there is the real possibility of competitors swinging out of the zone to collect 10 penalties. Careful observation and walking the fence through the 'eyes of the competitor' will enable the Fence Judge to recognise the danger and choose a position where the crucial line of the zone can be judged clearly and fairly. The best way to do this is to stand looking straight down the line like a linesman at Wimbledon Tennis Championships! It can be clearly seen when all four feet of the horse have crossed over the line.

[4] Penalty zone: FEI, Article 536 Para. 6.
[5] Penalty zone: FEI, Article 536 Para. 7.

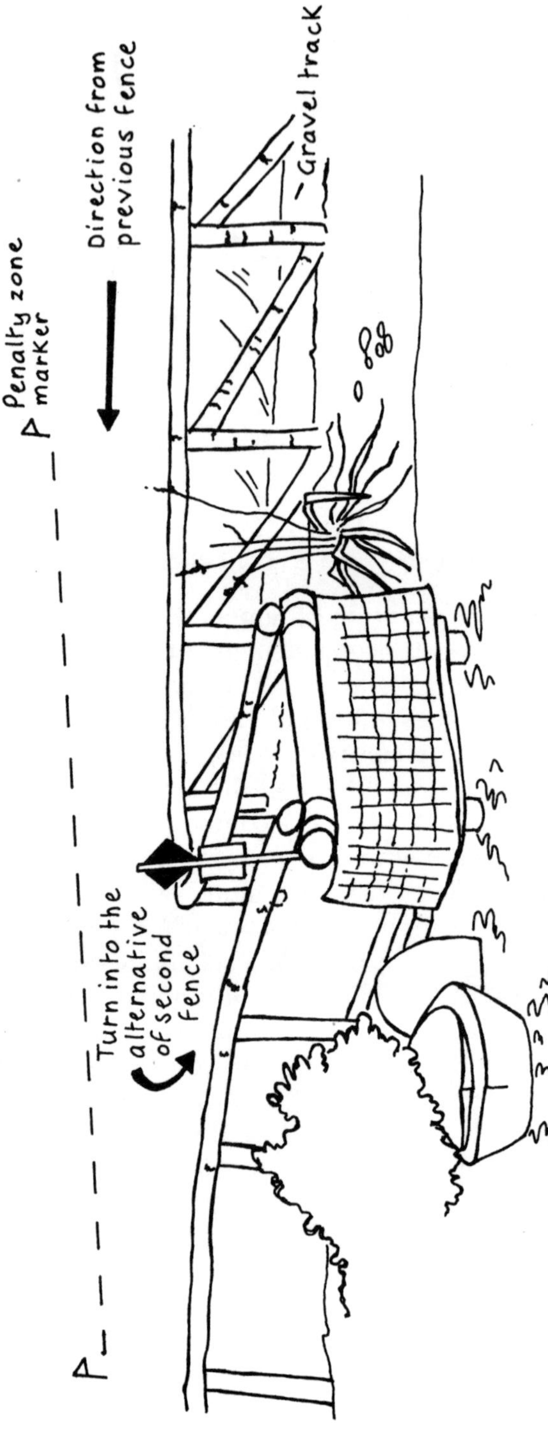

Figure 39. A 'close' turn between the alternatives of adjacent fences in a combined penalty zone.

CASE STUDY 15

Competition: *Olympic Games (CCIO ****)*
Fence: *Two separately numbered obstacles of a water complex with a combined penalty zone. Both fences had an alternative option.*

A first look at the complex about a week before the competition immediately raised a concern about that area of the penalty zone where riders would turn in order to present at the alternative fence into the water (Figure 39). There was clearly a possibility that competitors could leave the zone as they turned to present. As with most alternative routes, it was designed to be a time-waster, and the long track between the alternative fences was no exception. There was the added demand to pull back to a trot or at most a collected canter in hand in order to negotiate the bend before turning to face the second fence.

The only way to judge the zone was to have one Fence Judge at one of the flags marking the zone line before the approach to the alternative of the second fence. Two other members of the 'team' took it in turns in the intense heat to stand in position at the zone marker at the other end of this line. They were trained by the Fence Judge during the practice days before the event to judge this line with the Fence Judge. The diagram of this area shows that the line between the crucial penalty zone flags (which was not marked on the ground) formed a tangent with the curve of the track. The line between the flags was judged as a straight line with a person always at each end carefully watching each competitor as they rode through. The critical judgement was that all four feet had clearly to leave the zone before incurring penalties. There were a number of cases, in fact, where only two feet, off-fore and off-hind, left the zone and no penalties were incurred. If there was any doubt whatsoever concerning the fourth foot the benefit was always given to the competitor. With confirmation of 'Four feet' — 'Si, quatro. Salida zona' it was 10 penalties for leaving the zone.

In the event the concern was well founded, with 12 competitors leaving the zone at that critical point. During the day the Technical Delegate and later a member of the Ground Jury visited the fence to observe at first hand that the line was being judged as a straight line between the two penalty zone flags. This proved to be of vital importance when the Fence Judges were summoned by the Ground Jury at the end of the competition to give details of the manner in which each competitor had been judged and to submit the individual sketches made at the time of each transgression. Each diagram had been drawn immediately after the judges had walked and confirmed the track taken out of the zone before recording it. Once this was completed the marks left by the horse on the bare soil were trodden in so that fresh tracks could be seen clearly. Six nations lodged their individual objections with the Ground Jury. Their objections raised two essential points. One, that the dimensions of the penalty zone around the alternative route to the second fence was incorrect, and two, that riders were permitted to ride a curved route between the penalty zone flags in question.

Drawings of that area of the zone and the seond fence were produced by each competitor to substantiate the first point. Indeed, they had visited the obstacle throughout the afternoon to pace out distances and measure angles. It transpired, however, that they had taken their distances from the railings bordering the lake (approximately 8 metres) and not from the boundary flags of the obstacle which gave a generous dimension in excess of 10 metres (the minimum distance which a penalty zone should extend in front of an obstacle). The case for riding a curved track between the two zone flags in question proved to be a mistaken assumption on the part of the competitors. The opportunity to raise any queries of this nature is always available to competitors after they have walked the course prior to the competition. It is all too easy to be wise after the event.

After discussion, the arguments put forward in each case were dismissed by the Ground Jury and the 10 penalties awarded for leaving the zone were upheld.

The Ground Jury consists of a President and two members and is ultimately responsible for the judging of the event and for settling all problems which may arise during the time they are in 'office'. They are very experienced people, and have the responsibility for determining the outcome of objections against decisions made by technical personnel. This includes Fence Judges. After all the facts have been studied and discussed carefully, the Ground Jury may substitute their judgement for that of any judge. This may or may not be in favour of the competitor.

By way of a postscipt, only six competitors in the above case took the direct route − a solid curved gate with a downhill landing and a bounce over an upright wall into the lake. One rider fell, but promptly remounted and continued, while the other five went clear. Those competitors who dropped quickly down the slope on the alternative route, on to the gravel track which bordered the railings surrounding the lake, and pulled their horses right back were never in any danger of leaving the penalty zone.

For the Fence Judges it was one of the longest days in their judging experience. They were up at 3.30 in the morning in order to leave the hotel on the coast and drive the 70 miles up into the mountains and to be in position at the water complex by 6.30 a.m. This allowed for final detailed checks to be carried out before the first competitor set off on the course at 10 a.m. During this period, as the sun climbed higher into the sky, the green frogs which lived in the lake started up their chorus, as they had done on practice days. Once the first horse had gone through the lake there was not a sound from them for the rest of the competition. The last horse set off at 5 p.m. Once it had cleared the water complex the judges had to wait for the last score sheets to be collected and for the all clear to be given by Control so that they could leave their fences. Half way up the hill leading back to 'headquarters' where all the equipment was to be handed in, the frogs started up their chorus again. The lake was theirs once more. Two hours with the Ground Jury meant that it was too late to return to the hotel in time for supper. A super meal was enjoyed at the cross-country site before driving the 70 miles back, and the day finally ended around midnight.

11 · 'L' FENCES AND TIMED SECTIONS

The competitive career of many of the world's top riders began with the Pony Club.

Pony Club Trials are run under the same rules and scale of penalties as Official BHS Horse Trials, although there are two important additions to the rules. The cross-country course usually includes the old favourites such as a coffin and a water complex. Some fences may have an easier alternative to the more difficult 'main' fence, and the easier option is marked with the letter 'L' which has the same number as the main obstacle. These 'L' fences have an additional rule for the awarding of penalties.

In the first instance, competitors may choose to attempt the 'main' obstacle or the corresponding 'L' obstacle in much the same way as a rider may choose between the direct route and the alternative at a BHS trial. In Pony Club trials, however, to elect for the 'L' fence incurs 15 penalties.[1] In the case of a combination fence, they may change after jumping one or more of the 'main' elements to the next corresponding 'L' element. Once competitors have elected to take an 'L' fence they must continue to jump 'L' elements only and in the correct order. Competitors are not allowed to revert to the 'main' obstacle or any part of it once they have attempted an 'L' obstacle or an 'L' element in a combination fence. Reverting back to the 'main' obstacle entails elimination at that fence. Fence Judges do not verbally eliminate but record the incident on the score sheet. As with BHS Trials, the only time a Fence Judge eliminates a competitor verbally is after three refusals, run-outs or circles. A competitor is only awarded 'L' penalties once at a fence, so

---

[1] Pony Club Horse Trials, *Instructions to Fence Judges*: Judging 'L' Fences: Rule 3(c).

jumping, say, the three 'L' elements of an obstacle is still only 15 penalties, and not 45!

When a rider changes from the 'main' obstacle to a subsequent 'L' element, he does not have to go back and jump any 'L' elements when he has already jumped their corresponding 'main' element, although he may do so if he wishes.

CASE STUDY 16

Competition: *Pony Club One-Day Event*

Fence: *Water complex. The 'main' route consisted of five lettered elements (Figure 40): upright rails at (A), a drop into the water at (B), two steps up out of the water at (C) and (D), followed by a second set of upright rails at (E). The 'L' alternatives were made up of a gentle slope down into the water (A), a small step up out of the water (B) and a smaller set of rails (C).*

Figure 40. Water complex with 'L' alternatives. Both riders incur 15 penalties for taking the 'L' route.

Penalties, of course, are cumulative so a total of three refusals, for example, over 'main' or 'L' obstacles means elimination. It was not surprising that many competitors throughout the competition picked up penalties at this obstacle. One competitor managed to clock up a total of 135 penalties and was still entitled to continue! After a first refusal at 'A' of the main obstacle (20 penalties) it was cleared at the second attempt, followed by a second refusal at the drop into the water (40 penalties) which catapulted the rider out of the saddle and into the pond (60 penalties). Once re-united with her horse, the competitor then changed to the 'L' elements through the fence (15 penalties). Although the competitor had already jumped the corresponding 'main' element at 'A' at the second attempt, there were no further faults incurred for taking 'A' of the 'L' route. A character-building exercise if there ever was one!

Another variation to the rules as compared with those for BHS Horse Trials is the one regarding a horse resisting its rider. At Pony Club events a competitor is eliminated if the horse resists for 60 consecutive seconds anywhere on the course.[2] Fence Judges are asked to start timing as soon as they observe that a horse is resisting.

Hunter Trials are competitions run over a cross-country course. There are no dressage or showjumping phases as there are in eventing. There are usually classes for Novice, Intermediate and Advanced competitors and also a pairs class.

In Three-Day and Two-Day Events which include the complete endurance phase of roads and tracks and steeplechase, if two or more competitors finish on identical scores for the whole competition then the best score obtained on the cross-country (including time penalties) is the winner. If this has not divided the competitors into their individual placing then the competitor whose cross-country time was closest to the optimum time for the course will win. And after this the optimum time for the steeplechase is taken into consideration.

The main difference in comparison to the cross-country phase in eventing is that, in a Hunter Trial, if two riders finish on the same penalty score the fastest time wins.

This means that riders at Hunter Trials try to go clear in the

[2] Pony Club, Rule 4(a).

Figure 41. Timing competitors in the Timed Section.

fastest time possible. The real danger has been that riders often go far too fast for safety and there have been serious accidents in the past. To avoid this happening, many Hunter Trials now use a Timed Section. This is a section of the course which consists of a series of fences over which competitors are timed. When they are not in the Timed Section riders are not under any pressure to push on against the clock — they can go at their own pace. The obstacles in the section are usually arranged so that several turns are involved which again reduces the risk of competitors 'racing' over them.

Being in charge of a Timed Section means at the very least being in control of several watches to time riders in and out with, and timing sheets to fill in. At its most exciting there will also be the fences to judge as well. With, perhaps, five fences this will mean five score books! Judging a Timed Section can therefore be extremely hectic and demanding on your powers of concentration. The watches are ordinary stopwatches, so once a competitor enters the section and the watch is started, it must continue to run until the competitor leaves the section and the watch is stopped and the time taken recorded. It is important to remember to zero the watch again ready for use.

The trouble is that competitors all too often encounter problems in the Timed Section. A refusal means that the next horse is fast catching up and it is not unknown to have three horses in the section at the same time on their respective watches. Now comes the tricky bit! With run-outs and refusals occurring in the section, competitors often overtake each other. The judge doing the timing needs to watch very carefully and make sure that the correct watch is picked up to record any finishing time. A good method is to write down the competitor's number on a clip board and keep the watch with the clip board to avoid making a mistake. Once the time has been recorded for a particular rider, the number can be crossed off ready for the next one.

The judge will usually have a radio and should contact the start so that further competitors are prevented from starting if there are competitors in trouble in the Timed Section. As Timed Sections are usually early on in the course, some Trials will ask for the start to be informed as a competitor is about to leave the Timed Section before the next horse is set off. This avoids a 'build-up' of competitors in the Section.

The rules which govern Official Trials also apply to Hunter Trials in the main. So, for example, three refusals at an obstacle entails elimination. Most trials insist that competitors leave the course as soon as they have been eliminated. Others allow the riders to go on − with the result that some riders get in the way of others who are going clear. Odd riders flatly refuse to leave the course. At one such event, a competitor was eliminated in the Timed Section and refused, in spite of repeated polite requests, to leave or get out of the way of the following rider. Her retort was, 'If you think I've paid all this money to get only this far, you've got another think coming.' And with that she took a lead from the other competitor and finally disappeared out of sight, much to the relief of the Fence Judges. Although it was documented that a lead had been taken it was not crucial as the same competitor finally left the course after an elimination elsewhere!

In the pairs class, two competitors ride the course together. Penalties are cumulative, so that if both riders stop at a fence, it is two refusals. A third refusal by either of the horses means elimination of the pair. All too often the first horse puts in a stop and, of course, the second one promptly follows suit − 60 penalties. In the Timed Section the watch is started as the first horse enters and is stopped as the last of the pair leaves.

Some fences on the course will be selected as 'dressing' fences which can be placed anywhere on the course. This means that they must be jumped by the competitors together as a pair, that is with both ponies/horses abreast of each other. Any 'gap' between one horse and the next is penalised by, say, 5 penalties for anything in excess of a length. Individual Hunter Trials will vary on this. Some will award 2.5 penalties for half a length gap and 5 for a whole length. Some will give a time penalty. It has been said that Hunter Trials make up the rules to suit themselves. The whole idea behind 'dressing fences' is one of control, so that the pace of competitors is usually slowed down in order to meet the 'dressing fence' together. Shouts of 'Hang on − wait for me!' inevitably resound around the course.

12 · AN EVENT IN THE DAY OF A FENCE JUDGE: PUTTING IT ALL TOGETHER

The 'day' begins the previous evening. Everything is prepared and carefully packed. Top of the list is the checking of the contents of the Fence Judge's 'basket'. (At the end of the book I provide an appendix which details the contents of our 'basket'.) Although we can expect a packed lunch, we make up parcels of food to take with us as well. It is surprising how a long day at a fence out in the fresh air improves the appetite! The cool box is placed ready to put cold drinks and ice cubes in it in the morning.

Start time next day is around 5 a.m. This allows us to drive the 30 odd miles to the Trials and to walk the course before the Fence Judge's briefing in the main marquee at 8.30 a.m. It is great to walk the track early in the morning and return to the Land Rover for breakfast − a bacon roll and a cup of coffee. Walking the course, either the morning of the event or the day before, enables you to get a feel of the whole course and provides the opportunity to study the more demanding fences. In addition, it is surprising how it helps you to follow the Commentator when he waxes lyrical over the public address system during the competition. All the best commentators walk the course; that is, if they do not happen to have designed it.

This particular morning we set out with no certain knowledge of our fence. By the time we reach the finish we are confident that we can find our way directly to most of the fences on the course and know where we would park. Two fences in particular catch our eye. One, a combination, consists of a substantial upright followed by a drop into a sunken road, followed by a narrow arrowhead. The second, again a combination, has a fairly wide corner to be jumped as the direct route or rails in followed by rails out of the longer option. The direct line through both fences will require accurate and bold riding. We live in hopes of being given one of these obstacles to judge. While we enjoy breakfast the event begins really to come to life. Horse boxes are arriving, the odd competitor lungeing their horse, someone else trying to, and a few already making their way to the dressage arena. The weather is fine and the sky is clear. Briefing is at 8.30 a.m. and the first horse is due to set off on the cross-country phase at 10 a.m. We arrive in good time at the briefing to collect the set of flags, score books, timing watch and a radio. We are delighted to discover on this occasion that we have the arrowhead combination to judge and two fences beyond to report on the radio. Time then to meet up with old acquaintances and exchange news and gossip.

The briefing is good, direct and to the point. There are wise references to three of the more demanding fences and a spontaneous dash of humour which we had heard the week before 100 miles away. With the first horse due on the course at 10 a.m. the Technical Adviser asks us all to be at our fences by 9.40 to allow reasonable time for a radio check and to ensure that all Fence Judges are in position. The phase cannot start until they are. (In the same context the event may not start until the doctor and vet are on site.) Someone asks the inevitable question: 'What time does the last horse go'? There is a somewhat stony silence when the time of 5.30 p.m. is given. There are a lot of entries and it is going to be a long day.

Having walked the course we have no difficulty in driving straight to our fence after the briefing. Most fences can be reached by car although some, especially in wet conditions, can only be reached by a four-wheel drive vehicle. Judges are asked not to drive over the approach and landing areas of an obstacle. Certainly in soft going this will not do either any good. In addition, we already know the location of the fences before and after the one we are judging. We park under a magnificent oak and place all the equipment where it can be quickly and easily reached. The timing marker (a plastic road cone) is placed clearly in view some 100 paces before the fence and well to the side of the track riders will take from the previous fence towards ours. At one time we used a straw bale but spectators tended to move it around to sit on. After that we tried a wellington boot on a stake hammered into the ground but spectators often returned the boot to us thinking that it had been lost. Sometimes a natural feature can be used as a timing point, a tree or a bush for example. Anything will do as long as it is going to remain there for the duration of the competition. Where there is less than 100 paces between the previous fence and the one being judged then the landing side of the previous fence can be used to time from.

We introduce ourselves (Fence 9) to the judges on 8, 10 and 11 and arrange a system of signals with the judges, whose fences we are reporting on, to confirm penalties. Otherwise, if there is a doubt as to whether a competitor has incurred penalties it is best to report that they 'appear' to have had a refusal or whatever.

Then we check our obstacle to identify the cords which could be safely cut in the event of a horse becoming trapped on the fence. Both the upright rails at A and those of the arrowhead at C are secured with cord. Finally, a plan of the obstacle is drawn up with all the possible tracks a competitor might take through it. This is useful to refer to when an incident occurs, for example crossed tracks. It also identifies areas which must be kept clear of spectators and, as there is no roping around the fence, sharp vigilance will have to be kept. It also enables us to identify the safest route for the runners to take when they come to collect the score sheets.

The course is now open. We split up in order to judge the fence effectively and to cope with any dramas. One of us is positioned near the landing side of the last element and the other near the take-off side of the first. This gives full control of the obstacle with clear views all round.

A minimum of two people is normally required to judge and look after a fence. This is essential for those obstacles which are likely to have problems and for complexes or fences with alternative routes. At the higher levels of competition more people are required for these types of fence. An International Four Star Event will have a 'Team'. At the Olympic water complex (case study 15) the Team consisted of two FEI Fence Judges, a national judge of the host country, a radio operator and three 'helpers'.

At lower levels of competition it is possible for one person to be in sole charge of a fence and in these cases it will be a straightforward obstacle which is unlikely to have serious dramas.

The only reason one person may be used is because there are not enough to have two at every fence. It has been known for a pair of judges to be in charge of three fences, one of them a water complex, and also to report on a further two fences on the radio!

It can be a little nerve-wracking waiting for the first competitor to arrive at your fence, and always a relief if the first one goes clear. The first few horses are timed past the marker for practice and the reporting of competitors over the fences settles to a clear rhythm. Take-offs and landings need little attention as the going is good. There are the inevitable refusals at A and run-outs at the arrowhead, but otherwise the fence rides well and there are no accidents.

One incident we were privy to over the radio. The judge on the finish asked advice from Control when a rider passed on the outside of the boundary flags of the finish and headed straight back towards the horse boxes. Back came the dulcet tones of the Technical Adviser: 'If you fell strongly about it, I suggest that you find him, tell him he has not crossed the finish line — and then eliminate him for outside assistance the moment he does.' Of course, left to his own devices, which he was, the competitor failed to return within the time allowed for the course and was eliminated anyway.

Last horse on the course! We wait for the Pony Club runner to collect our last score sheet and we collect all the equipment up. Then, with equipment returned, we join friends at the back of

Figure 42. At the end of the day.

the Land Rover and exchange yarns over a well-earned drink.

The cross-country phase is the most influential of the three tests in eventing. The course and obstacles are designed as far as possible to obtain this degree of relative influence. A Fence Judge is privileged to be an important member of the entire operation involved in the sport, and similarly if you are a good Fence Judge the 'team' is privileged to have you as a member.

APPENDIX: CONTENTS OF OUR BASKET

First aid kit: for ourselves, which includes tweezers, for the removal of splinters which are very easily picked up from some fence poles, and fly repellent in summer.

Sturdy hammer: for those odd repairs to loose staples and nails.

Secateurs: in case the fence is a bullfinch which will inevitably need maintaining during the competition and which is always made of scratchy material.

Gardening gloves: repairing a bullfinch can play havoc with your hands!

*Sharp knife**:   to cut ropes securing poles if a horse becomes trapped on the fence.

Wire cutters: in case the fence poles are secured with wire.

Clip board: essential for the score sheets, although most Trials provide one for you.

Spare pencils: as you are bound to mislay the one provided even if it is attached by string to the clip board.

Pencil sharpener: to keep pencil sharp for the beautiful, clear diagrams of crossed tracks which you may need to draw.

Whistles: the Trial will provide you with one. However, we prefer our own which can be heard miles away and gives no one an excuse for saying that they could not hear it.

Lengths of twine: in case of loose dogs, and which inevitably needs replacing because no one ever returns it. (Hint: it is useful to collect the pieces of cut ropes off a fence when it has required dismantling as these make excellent 'leads'.)

A length of rope: only because this has come in useful, once, for pulling over a horse which had become cast up against the fence after the saddle had been removed. And for towing vehicles out of deep mud.

Two red flags: these have short sticks and can be easily tucked into a belt so that they are readily available in an emergency. The ones provided at the Trial are often on a metre of cane or have thick sticks.

Clear plastic bag: to cover the radio with if we are given one and it rains.

Binoculars: useful for spotting competitors' numbers. (And 'spying' on other Fence Judges.)

Leather punch: has come in useful for our own needs and also for those rare occasions when a rider's stirrup leather has split. A new hole punched and they are quickly on their way again and eternally grateful to you!

The BHS leaflet *Instructions to Fence Judges**: This is sent out in advance of the Trial for you to read and you are requested to study it and bring it with you. Why is this important item placed in the basket last, you may well ask! First, it is the last item placed in the basket because we are avidly reading it throughout the night! Secondly, it is the first item you require when you attend the briefing next morning.

(Spade*, rake*, yard broom, timing marker, umbrellas and wellington boots are already stashed in the back of the Land Rover where they tend to remain for the rest of the season.)

Note: Fence Judges are not expected to bring all this equipment, but experience has taught us how invaluable these items can be. Judges are requested to bring along all the items marked above with an asterisk.

BIBLIOGRAPHY

Regulations of the Fédération Equestre Internationale: *Rules for Three Day Events* (18th edition effective 1 Jan. 1992)
FEI Bulletin No. 12, 1992

The British Horse Society:
Horse Trials Group Rules, 1992 and 1993
Three Day Events − *Instructions to Fence Judges*, 1992
Horse Trials − *Instructions to Fence Judges*, 1993
Horse Trials − *Timing Instructions*, April 1991
Horse Trials − *Instructions to Radio Operators*, April 1989
The Pony Club Horse Trials, *Instructions for Fence Judges*, 1992

INDEX